HIS • • •
VERY

Paul' Epistle

to the Ephesians

By

NORMAN B. HARRISON, D.D.

Pastor, Bible Teacher and Evangelist

Author of

"His Salvation as Set Forth in the Book of Romans,"
"His in a Life of Prayer," "His in Joyous
Experience," "His Sure Return,"
"His Indwelling Presence,"
"His Peace"

Eighth Printing
23rd Thousand

"In the heavenlies in Christ Jesus"

THE HARRISON SERVICE
3112 Hennepin Avenue
Minneapois 8, Minnesota

The price of *this* book $1.25, Paper only

CONTENTS

His Very Own

To our friend. Dr. Norman B. Harrison,

S. E. C.

Sidney E. Cox

His ver - y own, His ver - y own, Won - der - ful grace in His
Word is made known; Chos - en by the Fa - ther, Pur - chased
by the Son, Seal'd by the Spir - it, I'm His ver - y own.

THE APPROACH

WHAT WE MAY EXPECT TO FIND IN EPHESIANS

The Epistle to the Ephesians marks a decided turn to higher, loftier levels of teaching in the progress of revealed truth and its correspondent experience in the New Testament.

The epistolary form of unfolding the truths concerning the Christian life is in itself the unique glory of the New Testament writings. Yet this fact is largely lost upon us to whom the form has come to be so familiar. What if Church truth had been dictated to us in an autocratic exercise of Apostolic authority! Instead it gently filters into our lives through these graciously inscribed letters.

Professor Moule has well said: "It (the use of the letter) is a suggestive remark, reminding us of that open communication and equal participation of revealed truth which is the prerogative of the later above the former dispensation; indicating too that the teacher and the taught are placed on one common level in the fellowship of truth. The Prophets delivered *oracles to the people,* but the Apostles wrote *letters to the brethren,* letters characterized by all that fulness of unreserved explanation, and that play of various feeling, which are proper to that form of intercourse. It is in its nature a more familiar communication between those who are, or should be, equals."

Now, what makes these reflections a fitting part of our approach to Ephesians is the fact that in this particular Epistle the Christian letter soars to its highest reaches as the vehicle for revealing the grace and truth of redemption.

Spiritual Preparation

Let no man think that he can gather the hidden riches of this Epistle, enter its inmost sanctum, scale its heights, or fathom its depths, aided only by the physical eye and the natural mind. It cannot be done. They belong to another realm, another order of reality.

It requires spiritual faculties and spiritual senses to perceive and grasp spiritual things when presented in their ultimate realities and relationships. Of this Paul explicitly warned the Corinthians, devotees, as they were, of earthly wisdom:

"The natural man receiveth not the things of the Spirit of God: for they are foolishness unto him: neither can he know them, because they are spiritually discerned" (1 Cor. 2:14).

We must have "the Spirit which is of God" to "know the things that are freely given to us of God," things which "the Holy Spirit teacheth, comparing spiritual things with spiritual" (1 Cor. 2:12, 13).

To no part of Scripture does this more truly apply than the portion into which we are now to adventure. As Dean Alford says in his introduction: "As the wonderful effect of the Spirit of inspiration on the mind of man is nowhere more evident than in this Epistle, so, to discern those things of the Spirit, is the spiritual mind here more than anywhere required."

To the one who will approach Ephesians in the attitude of humbly yielding to the necessity for heavenly wisdom, the mind quickened by His Spirit, the eyes of the heart enlightened (Eph. 1:18), there will burst from its pages, to be registered upon the retina of the soul, the most entrancing portrayal of life one may ever hope to have, short of being actually transported into heaven itself.

Historical Setting

For the historical background of the Ephesian letter we need to turn to Acts 19 and 20:17-38. From this narrative we learn that Paul was constrained to spend three years in this capital of heathen worship, the longest time given to any community. It was a memorable ministry. He reminds the Ephesian Elders "that by the space of three years I ceased not to warn every one night and day with tears."

The immediate result was a tremendous spiritual upheaval, which found practical expression in "many" bringing their books of magic, whose cost totaled a great sum, and consigning them to a huge public bonfire, "before all." The writer sums up the situation: "So mightily grew the word of God and prevailed" (Acts 20:19, 20). The entire city was stirred to an extent that alarmed the devotees of Diana, whose worship centered in Ephesus, with its temple and the image "which fell down from Jupiter," rousing them to riotous opposition (Acts 20:23-41).

And now, imprisoned at Rome, Paul is writing back to them this supernal message, sending it by Tychicus, along with his letters to Philemon and the Colossians.

The background sheds much suggestive light upon the lofty character of the Epistle to the Ephesians— heavenly beyond all other New Testament books. First: Paul's three years of resident ministry among them had enabled him to inculcate the higher spiritual truths, as with no other church, giving them a grasp and perception of truth which served to prepare them for such a written message. (So today, only certain churches, schooled in the things of the Spirit, could "receive" such a letter.) Second: The Ephesians made large claims for the celestial origin of Diana and her worship. This Epistle offers the antidote to such heathen claims, in the realities which are ours, "blessed with all spiritual blessings in the heavenlies in Christ" (1:3).*

The temple of Diana, moreover, grand in its proportions and magnificence—425 feet long by 220 wide and counted one of the wonders of the world—undoubtedly overshadowed and colored the whole life of the city. It must often have struck home with grief to the Apos-

---

* Some Biblical students question whether this Epistle was originally addressed to the saints "at Ephesus." Two main considerations are urged: (1) The fact that two of our best manuscripts do not contain the words "at Ephesus." (2) The Epistle is lacking in any personal reference to saints at Ephesus.

Offsetting these considerations are the following: 1—The absence of personal reference is open to a twofold explanation. The Apostle's habit in writing is to make the least personal reference to those whom he knows the best. The Ephesians were his intimate parishioners for three years. (The student should note that salutations are also lacking in 1 and 2 Corinthians, Galatians, Philippians, 1 and 2 Thessalonians, and 1 Timothy. Romans, a church unvisited by Paul, abounds in them.) Again, the lofty purpose of the Epistle prompts the desire to introduce no human personalities, lest they detract from the one central theme—the glorified person of our Lord Jesus Christ and our relation to Him. 2—The Epistle contains numerous correspondences to language used in addressing the Ephesian elders; e.g., "grace" (Acts 20:24, 32), "bonds" (Acts 29:22, 23), "counsels of God" (Acts 29:27), "redemption of the purchased possession" (Acts 20:28), "build up" and "inheritance" (Acts 20:32). 3—No other Church known to us could have appropriately been addressed in terms of such lofty teachings. 4—The margin of one of the two manuscripts in question does contain the words "at Ephesus." 5—This leads to the inference that the Epistle came to be used as an encyclical letter to neighboring Churches, in which case it would be natural for a copyist to omit the localizing "at Ephesus" from copies destined to be read in other Churches. (We have a parallel example in a manuscript in which "in Rome" (Rom. 1:7) is omitted, apparently to generalize its message for other readers.)

No Epistle so well lends itself to such generalization—"to the saints and faithful in Christ Jesus" anywhere and everywhere—as the one now before us.

tle's spirit.   Can the heathen gods boast a finer temple
than our own true God?   No, indeed.   The result of
his meditation, under the inspiration of the Spirit, is
this letter couched in terms of the Tabernacle and
Temple, as we shall see.   Believers are His Body and
Temple, surpassing any earthly building, made glorious
by His gracious purposes and presence in this "holy
temple in the Lord" (2:21).

Position Among the Church Epistles

Ephesians is fifth in the canonical order of Church
Epistles.   It is first of the three distinctively elevated
and spiritual in their tone and message—Ephesians,
Philippians, Colossians.   Without pausing to state our
reasons, rooted in the structure of Scripture and of nature, we give these seven Epistles the following suggestive arrangement:

God's Message
To the
Natural Man
Romans

To the *Carnal Man*	*To the* *Spiritual Man*
1 Corinthians	Ephesians
2 Corinthians	Philippians
Galatians	Colossians

In 1 Cor. 2:14-3:1 we have God's threefold classification of men: The Natural Man, The Carnal Man, The
Spiritual Man.

The NATURAL MAN needs Salvation.   Romans is addressed to his need, declaring as its theme that "the

Gospel is the power of God unto salvation to every one that believeth" (Rom. 1:16). This Epistle is a general introduction to all the writings that follow. It treats the entire sweep of man's problem and God's remedy. The Natural Man needs the new birth, the impartation of the life and nature of God. But even so, he is distressed to find his new nature checkmated by the old. He is in an intermediate, baffled state—the flesh lusting against the Spirit. He realizes that he is but a Carnal Man (Romans 7). Something more is needed. Only as he yields to the indwelling Spirit, and the "life in Christ Jesus" becomes dominant and regnant, only then is he victorious—the victory of the Spiritual Man (Romans 8).

The problems and perplexities of the Carnal Man, doctrinal and practical, occasion the two letters to the Corinthians, First and Second, and to the Galatians.

The position and privilege of the Spiritual Man, doctrinally and experimentally, are the concern of Ephesians, Philippians and Colossians.

Note, further, that the Epistles of the former group are addressed to the Church, the local Church whose problems peculiar to it are being considered. Those of the latter group are addressed to the saints, the individual believers, constituting the Church. The carnal Christian must needs find his life in the local church, whatever its condition. The spiritual Christian, while serving in some local church, finds his life "in Christ" and in Him rises superior to local circumstances.

Ephesians in Contrast with 1 Corinthians. The above arrangement sets Ephesians over against 1 Corinthians in contrasting relationship. To the Corinthians Paul says:

"And I, brethren, could not speak unto you as unto spiritual, but as unto carnal, even as unto babes in Christ. I have fed you with milk, and not with meat: for hitherto ye were not able to bear it, neither yet now are ye able. For ye are yet carnal: for whereas there is among you envying, and strife, and divisions, are ye not carnal, and walk as men?" (1 Cor. 3:1-3).

The problems of the Carnal Man, so fully dealt with in 1 Corinthians, find their full answer and antidote in the higher, spiritual levels of Ephesians. Here Paul addresses himself, without restraint, to the Spiritual Man, reminding the believer that he is a "New Man" in Christ Jesus.

We can but briefly trace this contrasting viewpoint as it affects two outstanding themes: "Wisdom" and the "Church."

GOD'S WISDOM VERSUS MAN'S WISDOM. First Corinthians is much occupied with wisdom. "Wisdom" and "wise" occur 25 times in the first three chapters. It is wisdom on the human level; wisdom such as the Greeks seek after. It can save no one, and the Christian who dotes upon it will never get beyond the carnal state. Ephesians is an exposition of wisdom that is heavenly and divine, the marvelous, expanding wisdom of God in redemption:

"To the intent that now unto the principalities and powers in heavenly places might be known by the church the manifold wisdom of God" (Eph. 3:10).

THE CHURCH AN ORGANISM VERSUS AN ORGANIZATION. Corinthians is addressed to the local church and the local church with its problems is always in view. Even when the church is pictured as the "one body" with "many members" it is to remedy the confusion and disorder over "spiritual gifts" at Corinth (1 Cor. 12). The appeal is to the organization. In Ephesians there is no organization in view. It is wholly concerned

with the Church as an organism, the Body of Christ,
united to Him by the Spirit, deriving its life from Him
as its Head, "walking" as the Head may direct.

Hence the bold, almost daring, declarations concerning the Church; that, being the Body of Christ, we are
"seated together in the heavenlies in Christ Jesus"
(2:6) and that God's purposes through her are "that
now unto the principalities and powers in the heavenlies might be known by the church the manifold wisdom of God" (3:10).

This leads us to note, further, the positional relationship between

ROMANS AND EPHESIANS. Romans is introductory
to the whole body of epistolary teaching. It expounds
the Gospel as "the power of God unto salvation to
every one that believeth, to the Jew first and also to the
Greek." The marvelous new relation of Jew and Gentile, both to each other and to Christ their Head, remains, however, a "mystery" which Romans merely
refers to in its very closing words: "the revelation of
the mystery, which was kept secret since the world
began, but is now made manifest" (Rom. 16:25, 26).
This "mystery" is reserved for exposition in Ephesians,
a treatise quite correspondent to Romans in its pro-
fundity of truth.

The progress from Romans to Ephesians may be
stated thus:

IN ROMANS: Christ is Crucified and Risen.
            We are Crucified and Risen *with* Him.

IN EPHESIANS: Christ is Crucified, Risen, In the
              Heavenlies.
              We are Crucified, Risen, In the
              Heavenlies *in* Him.

EPHESIANS AND COLOSSIANS, be it noted, fall under the same grouping. The striking similarity between them cannot escape one, even in the most cursory reading. Yet the viewpoint of each is distinctive. Ephesians shows us our position in Christ as His Body. Colossians bids us realize our completeness in Christ as our Head. The one supplements the other, thus:

IN EPHESIANS: We are the BODY of Him, the Head.

IN COLOSSIANS: He is the HEAD of us, His Body.

Seven Significant Words

Ephesians will be found to yield up most of its rich treasure in and through its use of the following words. They stand out on its pages as key words, unlocking for us the meaning of its message.

1. "GRACE." It occurs 13 times. So central is it that the Epistle may well be termed "the gospel of the grace of God," Paul's expression to the Ephesian Elders (Acts 20:24).

2. "SPIRITUAL." This (spirit or spiritual) also occurs 13 times. It defines the sphere of truth with which we are dealing as well as the sphere of life in which we are living, in the transcendent riches of this Epistle.

3. "HEAVENLIES." It occurs 5 times, each most significant (1:3, 20; 2:6; 3:10; 6:12). A plural noun in the Greek, the translators, in their zeal to make the meaning and wording complete, have inserted the word "places," thus converting the noun into an adjective—"heavenly places"; yet "the heavenlies" comprehend more than places in the lofty thought and language of this Epistle.

4. "MYSTERY." It occurs 5 times (1:9; 3:3, 4, 9; 5:32). A crucial word in Ephesians. Not something mysterious, but rather a secret, hidden with God and

held in reserve for its proper time of revealing. That time has now come as concerns the constituting of the Church and God's age-purposes centering in her.

5. "BODY." This word occurs 8 times. It embodies the heart and burden of the message throughout the Epistle. We are His Body. In this fact is found our position in Christ (Chap. 1-3). From this fact flow the duties of Christian living (Chap. 4-6).

6. "WALK." It also occurs 8 times. "Walk" is the correlative of "Body." It is the heart of the Epistle's appeal. If "body" is what we *are,* "walk" is what we must *do,* and that worthily of Him the Head.

7. "IN." It occurs 93 times (89 in Greek). It is the *biggest* word in the book. Moreover, the fact that it is more germane to Ephesians, permeating its entire thought, as is true of no other book of the Bible, speaks volumes for the lofty, spiritual nature of the message. It correlates with John 15. It is the Abiding Life in wondrous display, wondrously expounded. Our life is "in" Christ, in union with Him, to be lived in the practical unison that this relationship begets and implies.

A glance at these words rewards with the discovery of a remarkable fact, namely, that the first six naturally group themselves into pairs: "Grace" and "Spiritual" (each occurs 13 times) ; "Heavenlies" and "Mystery" (each 5 times) ; "Body" and "Walk" (each 8 times). They should as naturally be coupled in the mind of the student.

A Threefold Epistle

Ephesians is preëminently a threefold Epistle. Particularly should this be noted in these three respects:

1. Three Persons of Deity: Father, Son, Holy Spirit.

2. Three Tenses of Time: Past, Present, Future.
3. Three Classes of Men: Natural, Carnal, Spiritual.

His Very Own

Our title for this treatise finds its suggestion and warrant, first, in a single verse; second, in the real inwardness and intent of the entire Epistle.

Chapter one, verse four, reads, in perhaps its truest translation, "He chose us as HIS OWN" (Weymouth). He wanted us as His very own; and in redemption this is what we are.

The working out of this divine longing over us and desire toward us, what He did to bring it about, and what this means to us now that He has wrought it out for us and is working it out in us—all this is the marvelous story of Ephesians. There is no story like it anywhere. Throughout we see ourselves as "His Very Own." And being such, in intimate bonds, we can do no other than live and act as *His Very Own.*

A Fourfold Arrangement

The reader will note that each section is accorded a uniform treatment, consisting of

1. Outline.*
2. Chart.
3. Note.*
4. Comment.

We earnestly urge, for the student's own profit, that each section of the Epistle be read through, thoughtfully and prayerfully, with the *Outline,* before proceeding with the further features of elucidation.

---

* These features serve two distinct purposes: the *Outline* aims at an accurate analysis of the Apostle's thought; the *Note* seeks to elucidate the essential elements of his teaching.

CHAPTER I

THE MOST WONDERFUL STORY EVER TOLD

EPHESIANS 1

How we, or anyone, ever came to be Christians is the marvelous story with which the Epistle to the Ephesians begins. We thought we knew something of the influences and circumstances causing us to become believers in our Lord Jesus Christ unto life eternal, perhaps even to the time and place. But no! When we read this story we realize that we knew nothing about it; that the real story, the sources and forces making for our faith, go back into a dateless past with which we had nothing to do.

It is a wonderful thing to be a Christian, to have the experience of God's saving grace; it is still more wonderful to know how and why we are Christians, what makes it possible for anyone to be a child of God. That is the matchless story unfolded in Ephesians 1.

Three Prehistoric Narratives

It is a notable fact that three of the outstanding books of the Bible, preëminently great through the nature of their contents, preface their message with a prehistoric narrative. These records antedate the human race, reaching back beyond the realm of human knowledge and experience. This fact is incapable of explanation on any theory that, refusing to recognize God as the Author, reduces the Bible to the level of human litera-

16

ture. Moreover, these narratives exhibit a progression
in beautiful accord with the progress of revelation:

GENESIS—the antecedents of the Earth as the Home
of man.

JOHN—the antecedents of Christ as the Saviour of
man.

EPHESIANS—the antecedents of the Believer as the
Redeemed of God.

To me this last must ever be the most wonderful for
it sets forth, all unsuspected, my personal, spiritual antecedents, rooted back in eternity past—the genesis of a
soul, and that my very own, myself. Only now do I
know whence I came and how to account for myself.
Then the wonderment of the story is multiplied many
fold as it goes on to tell how the carrying out of its
eternal purposes and provisions on my behalf called
forth a special manifestation of the Godhead, Father,
Son, and Spirit, in grace and power. When analyzed
in *Outline* and *Chart*, this becomes the striking feature,
capturing the eye and captivating the mind and heart.

Outline

The Salutation, 1:1, 2.

    a. By Paul, the Apostle, by the will of God (1a).
    b. To the saints and the faithful in Christ (1b).
    c. From God and the Lord Jesus Christ (2).

      Conveying Grace and Peace.

I. Our Standing as Believers in Christ Jesus.
    The Threefold Work of the Triune God, 1:2-23.
    1. The Father's Part in Our Redemption, 1:3-6.

    Doxology—Ascription of praise to the **Father**
    "who hath blessed us with every **Spirit**-ual bless-
    ing in the heavenlies in **Christ**" (3).

a. He chose us in Him before the world began
(past) (4).

b. Whereby we have the "position of sons"
(present) (5).

c. And are assured of acceptance in the Beloved
(future) (6b).
To the praise of the glory of His grace (6a).

2. The Son's Part in Our Redemption, 1:7-12.

a. For us He procured redemption through His
Blood (past) (7).

b. In us He is working out His wisdom and
will (present) (8, 9).
Thus, "in the fulness of times," to consummate all things in Himself (10).

c. To us He assures an inheritance in Himself
(future) (11).
To the praise of His glory (12).

3. The Spirit's Part in Our Redemption, 1:13, 14.

a. Having prompted faith through the hearing
of the Word (past) (13a).

b. He has now sealed us as the Spirit of Promise
(present) (13b).

c. This is the "earnest" of our inheritance, until
full, final redemption (future) (14a).
To the praise of His glory (14b).

4. Paul's Prayer for the Believer's Fullness of Knowledge, 1:15-23.

a. Paul's faithfulness on their behalf (15, 16).

b. The intent of his prayer (17-23).
He prays for a spiritual revelation (17).
Through the enlightening of the heart's eyes
(18a).
That thus they may know in fullness (18b):

   (1) The hope of His calling (18c).
        (Cf. the work of the **Father**—1:3-6.)
   (2) The riches of the glory of His inherit-
        ance in the saints (18d).
        (Cf. the work of the **Son**—1:7-12.)
   (3) The greatness of His power to us-ward
        who believe (19a).
        (Cf. the work of the **Spirit**—1:13, 14.)
        The measure of that power (19b)—the
        power exercised in Christ's Resurrection
        (20a) and exaltation to God's right hand
        (**20b**) giving Him **Headship** over all
        things (21-23).
        (a) Governmental—now and hereafter
             (21, 22a).
        (b) Spiritual—constituting the Church
             His **Body** (22b, 23).

Note—The Body, here introduced, becomes the
theme of Chapter 2.

Chart: See following page.

THE THEME of the Epistle, we conceive to be, HIS
VERY OWN, since it is occupied with the intimate relationship, even mystical union, existing between Christ
and His Own upon earth. This union underlies and
determines all the teaching, doctrinal and practical—
the exposition and the exhortation.

TWOFOLD DIVISION. The Epistle divides at the middle: three chapters for the doctrinal; three for the
practical. First HIS VERY OWN are viewed as to their
STANDING—their Position which is perfect and constant, and of His providing; followed by their correspondent WALKING—their Condition, which is imper-
fect and variable, as measured by their Standing. The
WALK, in the necessity of the case, merges into a WAR-
FARE.

~ Ephesians ~
— HIS VERY OWN —

	STAND-ING			WALK-ING		WAR-ING
	CHAP. 1	CHAP. 2	CHAP. 3	4:1-5:20	5:21-6:9	6:10-24
	AS HIS **BELIEVERS**	AS HIS **BODY** 1:22-23	AS HIS **BUILDING** 2:19-22			
FATHER { CHOSE ADOPTS / WILL ACCEPT } 1:3-6						
SON { PURCHASED ENLIGHTENS / WILL INHERIT } 1:7-12						
SPIRIT { SAVED SEALS / WILL CLAIM } 1:13,14						
Prayer for **R**evelation / **P**ower of **R**esurrection		**AMEN**			**B**RIDE—TO BE	**AMEN**

IN HIM — *Our Standing in Heaven*   IN US — *His Walking on Earth*

OUR STANDING AS HIS BELIEVERS is before us in Chapter 1. It is a standing that is secured wholly by the effectual working of

FATHER, SON AND SPIRIT in wondrous *pre*creation concert and covenant. This fact is the basic theme and teaching of the Epistle; from it all else unfolds. Their efficacious work in redemption spans from eternity past to an assured eternity future.

THREEFOLD AND THREE TENSE. With beautiful symmetry the work of each person of the Godhead is presented as threefold in character, covering, from the human viewpoint, the three phases of time, past, present, future—all time, merging at either end into eternity.

THE INTENT OF PAUL'S PRAYER, with its attendant teaching (1:15-23), is set forth in the last space of this initial column of the chart.

The Salutation, 1:1, 2

Note

THREE POINTS OF APPROPRIATENESS, in which this Salutation is specially suited to introduce the message that follows, should be noted by the reader.

(1) "PAUL AN APOSTLE BY THE WILL OF GOD" (1:1a). Nowhere is the will of God so exalted, yet so wondrously linked with Grace. Ephesians is an exposition of the sovereign will of God as the sufficient explanation, the beginning from which, the end toward which, the redemption of Grace proceeds. Paul, knowing himself to be an apostle by the will of God, would have every believer know that he is such by the same will.

(2) "TO THE SAINTS AND FAITHFUL IN CHRIST

Jesus" (1:1b) is a twofold designation correspondent
to the twofold division of the Epistle.

"Saint" is God's name for every believer. Meaning
"holy" or "set apart," it refers to our Standing in
Christ. Applied to the most unworthy (e.g., 1 Cor. 1:2
—not "called to be saints" but simply "called saints,"
though so reprehensible in conduct), God would have
us realize that sainthood is equally the position of all
believers, because that position is "in Christ." Cf.
Ephesians 1-3.

"Faithful" is the description of the believer in living
true to his saint-standing in Christ. Having believed
God as to his set-apart position as a believer, his faith
makes faithful in a correspondent Walk. To apprehend the former is to succeed in the latter. Cf. Ephesians 4-6.

(3) "From God our Father and the Lord Jesus
Christ" (1:2). No second "from" in this phrase. God
and Christ are one, the one source of "Grace and
Peace." This is not merely a tribute to the deity of the
Son, coequal with the Father. It serves to set before
us His exalted position with the Father, yonder "in
the heavenlies," a position to which Ephesians traces
the lofty benefits and blessings unfolded throughout.

Grace and Peace (1:2) is the greeting common to
all of Paul's Epistles. His gospel is always labeled
"Grace"—God's undeserved favor, nothing of desert
on our part. "Grace and Peace"—never the reverse,
either doctrinally or experimentally. God does not offer
peace apart from grace. One çannot experience peace
until he has accepted of grace.

Comment

"In Christ Jesus," greeting us in these opening
verses and occurring (it or its equivalent) no less than

14 times in Chapter one alone, is the key to all that
this Epistle contains for us. Every believer, because
baptized by the Holy Spirit into the body of Christ
(1 Cor. 12:12, 13), is "in Christ." In union with
Christ all that is in Christ is his because he is in Him,
in wondrous mystic identification. "In"—simplest of
words yet mighty in spiritual import. What is "in"
Christ, only eternity can unfold. What is ours "in"
Christ, now, of present standing, enrichment and empowering, yet continuing on into eternity, all that we
are and have in Him—this greets our gaze, stirs our
spirits, warms our hearts, steadies our steps throughout the pages of this heaven-born message. Who can
remain unchanged through studying and submitting
heart and life to its teaching!

Our Spiritual Life-Story, Told in Terms
of the Triune God, 1:3-14

These verses are all one sentence, the longest in all
Scripture and doubtless in all literature (see R.V.).
There is a reason. Into them is woven the most thrill-
ing story of spiritual biogenesis, in the telling of which
there is no place to stop; and this is so because the three
Persons involved are inseparable, both in their being
and in their activity.

Scripture's Greatest Doxology, 1:3

Note

BLESSED—BLESSED—BLESSING. "Blessed," literally,
is "well-spoken of." As we contemplate the gracious
wonders of redemption God our Father must ever be
"spoken well of" by His redeemed ones—blessed out of
overflowing hearts. The three words of blessing are
readily associated with the three Persons to whom re-

demption is about to be attributed in its: 1—conception; 2—execution; 3—application.

THE FATHER, SON AND SPIRIT are all here in this verse, by anticipation of the unfolding of their work in vv. 4-14. The Father planned and originated "every spiritual blessing." They are ours "in Christ," by whom we were redeemed. And they are Spirit-bestowed; spiritual, in that they emanate from the Holy Spirit.

IN THE HEAVENLIES. A phrase we meet at the outset because, while occurring but five times, it is a masterkey to the meaning of the Epistle. It is found nowhere else in Scripture. (Cf., however, John 3:12.) Briefly, it is of double significance:

(1) The Origin of "every spiritual blessing" is "in the heavenlies." Our Father is there (Matt. 7:11). From there our Lord and Saviour came (John 6:33, etc.). From there the Spirit came (Acts 2:2-4). But above all Christ is there, continuously, throughout this age, seated on the right hand of God, in the place of all-power. Our life is "in Him" (1 John 5:11); likewise, every other spiritual blessing whatsoever.

(2) The Nature of New Covenant blessing. Our Christ has triumphed in both spheres—the earthly and the heavenly. "All power (authority) is given unto Me in heaven and in earth" (Matt. 28:18). In heaven, then, where He is today, He is exercising Himself for the supply of our needs while we still live upon the earthly level. Were it not for this fact, spiritual life (we having been "born from above") would be an impossibility in a nonspiritual atmosphere. Man cannot live in water, except as air, his native element, is supplied to him from the upper level. Thus our heavenborn nature requires a constant supply of heaven-sent

blessing. The relation "in Christ" that secures this to us, it is this that Ephesians sets forth. The result of this relationship is just as the song expresses it:

> "Moment by moment I'm kept in His love;
> Moment by moment I've life from above."

EVERY SPIRITUAL BLESSING, however, does not mean spiritual as opposed to practical, material or financial. It means "Spirit-bestowed." It means that the above provision for our need is carried out by the Spirit —the Holy Spirit, proceeding from the Father and the Son.

He makes the plan operative. And while our essential, fundamental, "nature-al" need, as children of God, is in the realm of the spiritual—that without which we cannot live—His concern reaches out to the outermost rim of conscious need. The Father's love assures that He will "with Him freely give us all things" (Rom. 8:32). His great promise for "every need" has a setting that is outward and physical, causing us to know that His "spiritual" care for us is intensely practical. "My God shall supply every need of yours according to His riches in glory in Christ Jesus" (Phil. 4:19, R.V.).

"IN CHRIST." This last phrase is the sum of it all, the essence of the wonderful story committed to Paul to tell us through Ephesians—that story reduced to, concentrated into, two words, "In Christ." That Christ, once dead, is now alive; once on earth, is now in the heavenlies. Not merely "heaven," but "the heavenlies," involving all spiritual riches and realities, the revealed content for us of heaven. And we are there in Him.

"In Christ"—in union with, and resulting identification with Him—"every spiritual blessing" is ours. "In Christ" comprises our whole spiritual biography, its alpha and omega: our crucifixion to the old; our resurrection to the new; our walk in newness of life; our access to the Father in prayer; our strength for service; our sufficiency under trial; our glorification at last with His glory. In Christ—"the world, or life, or death, or things present, or things to come; all are yours; and ye are Christ's; and Christ is God's" (1 Cor. 3:22, 23).

Comment

A Doxology of Praise. The Psalms begin with "Blessed." So does Ephesians. The Psalms perennially grip us because they bear up to God, on wings of the loftiest aspirations of the soul, our praise and thanksgiving for His unceasing, ever wondrous benefits. It is so with Ephesians. The Apostle is fairly overcome by the depth of his emotion of gratitude, rising in a stream of praise, uninterrupted through this longest of sentences. It cannot stop short of praise to Father, Son, and Spirit, glorifying each for His marvelous hand in redemption.

It is fitting, then, that this expression take a somewhat poetic form, akin to the psalm. "The first chapter has, so to speak, a liturgical, psalmodic character, being, as it were, a glowing song of praise of the transcendent riches of the grace of God in Christ, and the glory of the Christian calling" (Schaff). So we have:

1:3-6	{ Tribute to God the Father { "To the praise of His glorious grace"
1:7-12	{ Tribute to God the Son { "To the praise of His glory"
1:13, 14	{ Tribute to God the Spirit { "To the praise of His glory"

The Trinity in Christian Experience. Some people seem to look upon the Trinity as having to do only with theology. They regard it as a sort of dry subject of speculation. But not so. Mentioned as a theme in verse 3, it is expanded into a portraiture lit up with all the warmth and color of human experience. The Triune God has stepped into the heart experience of men. Are we saved? Are we rejoicing in redemption, in restored relationship with God? It is because of what God the Father has done, supplemented by what God the Son has done, supplemented by what God the Spirit has done. Looking into this picture, listening to this story, we realize the practical values of the Trinity in terms of experience. We see that a unitarian God never did, nor could, save man; that man knows redemption only as he receives it through the Persons of the Trinity, successively manifested in their respective work for our salvation.

OUR HIGH-PRIEST IN THE HEAVENLY TABERNACLE. We shall not uncover the treasures of Ephesians nor make them ours except as we see that its teaching is couched in terms of the Tabernacle, or Temple. Christ, our High-Priest, His atonement accomplished on Calvary, has passed with the Blood of Atonement into the Holy of Holies; not here upon the earth, the mere pattern of the true, but "into heaven itself."

"For Christ entered not into a holy place made with hands, like in pattern to the true; but into heaven itself, now to appear before the face of God for us" (Heb. 9:24, R. V.).

As the High-Priest entered the Holy of Holies, acting representatively for the whole people of God and bearing upon his shoulders the names of the twelve tribes engraven on the precious stones of his breastplate, thus in his person carrying them into the presence of God, so in the person of Christ we, truly united to Him, are presented and accepted as "holy and without blemish before Him"; i.e., "in His presence" (vs. 4). In Him we are not only *presented,* we are veritably *present*—He has "made us sit together in the heavenlies in Christ Jesus" (Eph. 2:6).

And now, to be specific, yet perhaps only suggestive, let us ask ourselves what is "in the heavenlies" for us, as pictured in its earthly pattern, the Holy of Holies of the Tabernacle.

There is found but the one piece of furniture, the Ark, two-natured, typifying our Lord Jesus Christ in His deity and humanity. In it—the recurrent phrase of Ephesians is "in Him": 1—The Law, "broken" by man, perfectly "kept" in Him; 2—The Manna—an omer full, i.e., a man's daily portion, suited to his day-by-day needs; 3—Aaron's rod that budded, typically teaching that Christ by His resurrection has been forever established in His High-Priestly position, and having on the day of His resurrection called us "brethren," He is now gone into the heavenlies as the pledge of the day He will "bring many sons into glory" (Heb. 2:10).

Upon the Ark was the Mercy Seat, over which was the Blood of Atonement and the overshadowing Living Presence, the Cherubim. The Blood "covers" the broken Law, changing the throne of the universe from an otherwise Judgment Seat to a Mercy Seat for this Age of Grace. And the Living Presence is there (whatever else is typified) administering the affairs of the universe upon the principles of Calvary and its finished work, exalted to administrative authority in the Glory.

One further feature of the Ark, embodying the essential teaching of Ephesians, is found in the staves, which were "not to be taken from it." By them it was carried in the midst of God's people in all their journeyings. While its position was in the Glory Room, giving His people their "standing" before Him (cf. Eph. 1-3), its practical design was for a continual "walking" in them and with them (cf. Eph. 4-6). It thus mirrors forth the main features of the Epistle, taken in its entirety.

Scanning now the verses we are about to study, we find enumerated the following as making up the "every spiritual blessing" of our standing in Christ: Chosen (4); Sanctified (4); Foreordained (5); Adopted (5); Accepted (6); Redeemed (7); Forgiven (7); Enriched (8); Enlightened (9); Inherited (11); Sealed (13). All else in the first three chapters flows out from these.

1—The Father's Part in Our Redemption, 1:4-6

Note

God the Father planned it, long before we were on the stage of action. Note the past, present and future aspect of His work.

"CHOSE US IN HIM"—in the past (1:4). The form of the Greek verb gives it the sense, "chose us for Himself." This is very sweet and very significant in the study of the doctrine embodying this word, *i.e.*, Election.

How far in the past did He choose us? "Before the foundation of the world." It was no after-thought with God; nor was my relationship to Him. My name was upon His heart prior to any concern for the world. He leads me to believe that but for this preplanned relationship the world would not have been. First the Bride selected for the Son; then the home for her.

And this act of choosing us, yonder before all things, was "in Him," the Son. This could be so because the Son, before the beginning, had given Himself in solemn covenant for the work of redemption. He is "the Lamb slain from the foundation of the world" (Rev. 13:8). The decree that swung the worlds into being set up the cross in the heart of the Son.

Chose us for what? Not for salvation merely, but for something far more glorifying to Himself and satisfying to us—"that we should be holy and without blame in His presence." God's electing grace is misjudged when we stop short of its full, enriching intent:

> "Ye have not chosen Me, but I have chosen you, and ordained you, that ye should go and bring forth fruit" (John 15:16).
> "God chose you from the beginning unto salvation in santification of the Spirit and belief of the truth" (2 Thess. 2:13, R. V.).
> "For whom He foreknew, He also foreordained to be conformed to the image of His Son, that He might be the firstborn among many brethren" (Rom. 8:29, R. V.).

"Foreordained us to the Son-Position" (1:5). This is our present standing—"Beloved, now are we the sons of God" (1 John 3:2). "Children" refers to our birth; "sons" to our legal status. This latter is fully secured to us by adoption. It is mine now; but it was secured to me by His determining purpose that, having picked me for Himself, chosen me for His very own, He should have what He had chosen. Such is the intent of foreordination—the will to carry out His choice.

So the case stands thus: Before ever I had the chance, either in Adam or by my own wilful act, to take the position of a sinner, showing myself wholly undeserving, He had given me the position of a son, setting me down in His family register, *His Very Own*, a "son to Himself." This it was His "good pleasure" to will. Then it must come to pass. Upon what wonderful security my salvation was made to rest!

Assured of Acceptance in the Beloved (1:6). This is present experience that finds its fulfillment in a future prospect. We are now accepted in the Father's presence, in and through our High Priest. Therefore our boldness of approach in prayer (read Heb. 10:19-23). Every such experience of acceptance in prayer is the pledge and foretoken of the day when He who is "able" actually will "present us faultless before the presence of His glory with exceeding joy" (Jude 24).

"TO THE PRAISE OF HIS GLORIOUS GRACE" (1:6) is the goal of His selecting, electing love. Its terminus is not ourselves, but Himself; not our salvation, but the praising, publishing, extolling of His grace in all its heavenly glory. This purpose will be made manifest

"When He shall come to be glorified in His saints, and to be admired in all them that believe" (2 Thess. 1:10).

Comment

ELECTION, as a most precious doctrine of Scripture, will be little appreciated until we see: 1—It concerns always and only God's people. It explains why we are His. We did not choose Him; He chose us (John 15:16). It is never applied to others. Men are not elected to a state of reprobation or separation from God. The word is incapable of such a use. 2—Christ is the first Chosen One, the Elect of God—Isaiah 42:1-7. Then "He chose us in Him." Reader, you must ponder this well: do so before proceeding further. 3—Then it follows that He elected us, chose us, called us to a life of separation (a) "from" the world, the unseparated mass of men, (b) "unto" Himself and a life in keeping. (Cf. John 15:19; 17:16; Eph. 1:5). Every marriage ceremony is a picturing of the same twofold separation, namely, from all others unto the one beloved.

FOREORDINATION is, so to speak, God's Enforcement Act whereby what He has determined for us is carried out. It operates through His sovereign "will" (1:5). It ensures that what He has prepurposed for us shall not be nullified, but shall come to pass.

Foreordination and Free-Will are the old irre-
concilables; yet, like two parallel lines that meet at in-
finity, they harmonize in God, and viewed from eternity we will find in them no conflict. Difficulties will
largely disappear and our thinking become clear if we
can but realize that Foreordination concerns only God's
people, that so far as every man in the world is concerned he is free to accept Christ, and not only free, he
is invited and urged to do so, the ground for which is
the all-inclusive work of Christ; the fact that the Son
of God became incarnate, "That He by the grace of
God should taste death for every man" (Heb. 2:9).

The solution, in other words, lies in the two distinct
viewpoints of the two classes: outside of Christ the
man is concerned only with Free-Will. The Gospel in-
vitation is his. He can and should accept. But having
accepted, once he is "in Christ," his viewpoint changes
and he sees a wondrously deeper reason for his step—
he sees now why he accepted.

To illustrate. Let the Gospel be represented by a
church building. Its public signboard reads: "For God
so loved the world, that He gave His only begotten Son,
that whosoever believeth in Him should not perish, but
have everlasting life" (John 3:16). The passerby, attracted by it, approaches the steps, only to read over the
doorway: "Whosoever will, let him take the water of
life freely" (Rev. 22:17). He enters. Is he not bidden
so to do? Once within, his eye rests upon the amazing
statement, emblazoned on the inner wall: "Chosen in
Him before the foundation of the world" (Eph. 1:4).
He has willed with God. He now knows what he
could never have known otherwise. He sees the eternal
reach of his decision, back in the gracious, eternal will
of God. He knows that he came because the Father,
having chosen him, "drew" him (John 6:44). Yet—

who can point to a man on the outside that may not have a like experience?

A further illustration, radically different: the relation of the engine to the roadbed. Evidently the roadbed is a predetermined mapping out of the engine's life and destiny. Yet the engine is free to move upon the plane of its appointed tracks. Yea, only as it is true to them has it any real freedom. It is separated unto them from all the broad expanse on either side. So is the child of Grace, chosen in Christ.

2—The Son's Part in Our Redemption, 1:7-12

Note

The Father having PLANNED our redemption (4-6), the Son actually PROVIDED it, as we are now to see. That the plan involved another Person to carry it out is intimated in the closing of verse 6—we are "accepted in the Beloved." And why called Beloved? Jesus explains: "Therefore doth My Father love Me, because I lay down My life, that I might take it again" (John 10:17). Oh, the depth of the covenanted coworking of the Father and the Son for our redemption! He has thereby "translated us into the kingdom of the Son of His love," a love that will be the marvel of eternity.

REDEEMED US BY HIS BLOOD (1:7, 8). Redemption may mean merely deliverance but usually, as here, it is deliverance by means of a price paid. The price is "His blood." This price-paying Jesus Himself stated to be His aim and purpose: "The Son of man came not to be ministered unto, but to minister, and to give His life a ransom for many" (Matt. 20:28). Remember: "The life is in the blood" (Lev. 17:11). In Jesus' blood was a wholly pure, stainless life—the price He gave for us.

The result is "the forgiveness of sins." God had said
"Without shedding of blood is no remission" (Heb.
9:22). Ten times in Leviticus alone he connects the
atonement of blood, with the forgiveness of sins. God
knows no other way. But He does know this way. It
has been His way from the beginning. By every animal, innocent and unblemished, slain in sacrifice according to His direction, He was saying, "So is My Son
going to die"; until, one day, John pointed his finger
and said, "Behold" (Look, there He is), "the Lamb of
God that taketh away the sin of the world" (John
1:29). And on Calvary, His life poured out, in the
triumph of eternal purpose achieved, our Lord Jesus
Christ exclaimed: "It is finished" (John 19:30).

REVEALS TO US HIS WILL AND PURPOSE (1:9, 10).
The word "redeem" has to do with slaves, who are
bought and sold. Such we were, "the slaves of sin."
But now we are the free-born of God, of His own
family and household. In our new position and with
our new endowment—"we have the mind of Christ"
(1 Cor. 2:16)—He is able to take us into His intimate
confidence, making known to us what was necessarily
hidden from us ("mystery") hitherto.

"Henceforth I call you not servants; for the servant knoweth not what
his Lord doeth: but I have called you friends; for all things that I have
heard of My Father I have made known unto you" (John 15:15).

This revelation of His will, the purposings of His
good pleasure, comprehends the familiar matters of the
"management of the house"—for such is the literal
meaning of "dispensation" in the Greek (10a). The
new house, which we have become (see 2:19-22), the
mystery of whose make-up is unfolded in Chapter 3—
His highest purposings henceforth unfold in and
through the management of this house. So He has

much to tell us, in confidence and glad expectation, of
"the fulness of times," the rounding out of the seasons,
brought to their purposed fulfilment in the summing
up of all things, heavenly and earthly, in Christ. Thus
He floods our present with an enamoring prospect of
what we are to be "in Him" in glorious consummation.

OUR INHERITANCE—HIS HERITAGE (1:11). "In
Him" we, and He, have a glorious future in prospect.
It is the inheritance upon which we, and He, are to
enter. The Greek word, occurring only here, means
"we were allotted," harking back to the method whereby the tribes of Israel came to possess their inheritance
in Canaan. But the passive form is capable of a double
meaning: "We were allotted *to* a possession," or "We
were allotted *as* a possession." The Authorized Version
represents the first view; the Revised, the second. Both
convey the teaching of Scripture. Taken together, the
one enriches the other.

(1) "We have obtained an inheritance"—we who
were outcasts, stripped of all righteousness, deserving
of nothing. And what an inheritance it will be! "Heirs
of God, and joint-heirs with Christ" (Rom. 8:17).
"All things are yours; and ye are Christ's; and Christ is
God's" (1 Cor. 3:21, 23). A boundless inheritance—
the entire universe!

(2) "We were made a heritage"—that which the
Lord Jesus will inherit, as His covenanted right, in the
day when He makes up His jewels. It was for this joy
set before Him that He endured the Cross, despising
the shame, His eye was upon us, whom He was pur-
chasing for His possession, for *His Very Own*. It is in
us as His heritage that His day will be magnified:
"When He shall come to be glorified in His saints, and
to be marvelled at in all them that believed."

Who would not rejoice in His foreordaining grace, when once he has seen this as its glorious goal, guaranteed to us by His sovereign "purpose," wrought out "after the counsel of His will" (11b), to the intent "that we should be to the praise of His glory" (12a).

Comment

Redemption Liberates. When Christ redeemed us He reversed our standing completely—from the standing of slaves to the liberty of sons. A progression of words embodies the progress of experience: 1—The primary word "to redeem" means "to buy in the slave-market." It is there our Saviour found us and stooped to claim us. 2—With a prefix, *ex,* the word means "to buy *out* of the slave-market," thereby serving notice that we are no longer for barter—we are *His Very Own.* 3—A third word means "to loose"; He sets us free from all enslavement. It is thus that we are ushered "into the glorious liberty of the children of God." Let the redeemed of the Lord so live as to joyously appropriate and daily demonstrate "the freedom wherewith Christ hath set us free."

Christ Illuminates. In the New Birth He bestowed upon us His mind. Now He quickens that mind by His Spirit, flooding it with light, filling it with the knowledge of Himself and His purposes of Grace and Glory. To this end He bids us to abide in Him and let His words abide in us (John 15:7). This is preeminently the believer's present-age occupation. The aspiration of the Apostle's heart, "That I may know Him," largely accounts for the glorious reaches of revelation in his writings and experiences. It is His purposed preparation, now, in the primary grades, for the university of unending communion with Himself.

Our Prospect Allures. Scripture designs the picturings of Glory to promote our separation unto Him, here and now, in its prospect. How the heart of the saints in all ages has been ravished with the hope of the inheritance held out to them in His Word! What we are is wonderful; but to think of what we are going to be—how very wonderful!

"Beloved, now are we the sons of God, and it doth not yet appear what we shall be: but we know that, when He shall appear, we shall be like Him; for we shall see Him as He is. And every man that hath this hope in him purifieth himself, even as He is pure" (1 John 3:2, 3).

Like Him, then manifested with Him in His likeness, that He may be marvelled at in us as the heritage of His redeeming love. How unspeakable! How the lure of it all lays hold of our hearts for holy living.

3—The Spirit's Part in Our Redemption, 1:13, 14

Note

THE SPIRIT PROMPTED FAITH UNTO SALVATION (13a). No explanation of our salvation is complete that omits the ministry of the Holy Spirit. How came it? The Father PLANNED and PURPOSED it; the Son PROVIDED and PURCHASED it; the Spirit APPLIED it, in that He PERSUADED us to appropriate it.

But saving faith has the Lord Jesus Christ for its object. Hence the office work of the Holy Spirit for this age is that of holding before us, playing up, the person and saving work of Christ, that we may believe upon Him. "He shall not speak of Himself"; "He shall take of Mine and show it unto you" (John 16:13, 15).

To illustrate this relationship: A friend tells of walking the streets of Philadelphia one dark midnight during the war, when his attention was attracted to a beautiful flag on the top of a tall building, made visible and beautiful against the inky sky by search lights so

placed upon the roof that they played their beams upon
the folds of the flag. In their light it was seen. Nineteen hundred years ago God flung to the world the
flag of His salvation, the Cross of Calvary; and ever
since the Holy Spirit has been flooding it with light to
arrest our attention and arouse in us a longing for Him,
whispering, "Only believe and you shall be saved."

HE SEALS US AS HIS OWN (1:13b). Once we have
believed, the Spirit proceeds to secure His right in us.
This is His sealing work. The word "seal" has a threefold usage and significance, as follows: 1—A FINISHED
TRANSACTION, unchangeable with the stamp of authority, as when a notary public stamps a deed or any docu-
ment with the government's seal. 2—A MARK OF
OWNERSHIP, as when cattle or sheep upon the range
are branded, establishing the owner's rights and identi-
fying his property. 3—A GUARANTEE OF SAFE DE-
LIVERY, as when a package or car is sealed by the express company, forbidding any one's tampering with it
short of its destination. In each and all of these
respects are the saved of the Lord sealed with His
Spirit's gracious and sufficient sealing.

HE WILL CLAIM US AS HIS PURCHASED POSSESSION
(14). Called the "Spirit of Promise," the pledge of a
better and more perfect work, in His present gift to us
and inworking in us. He is but the "earnest" of the
divine purpose to claim in complete possession that
which He has purchased. Elsewhere we read of the
"First-fruits of the Spirit," in anticipation of the final
harvest. So here, He is the "Earnest money," God's
down-payment in our purchase, serving both to settle
the transaction and to bind Him to carry it to a full
and final settlement.

Comment

WE ARE SAVED BY THE SPIRIT. Do we realize this fact? Birth by the Spirit is the only entrance into the kingdom. Short of this there is no salvation. All that the Father has done; all that the Son has done—in all of this there is no salvation for one single soul except it be supplemented by the gracious work of the Spirit. What the Father planned and purposed for us; what the Son purchased and procured for us—all is made over to us in personal possession, in perpetuity, by the Spirit's part in salvation. By Him the promises of redemption are coined into the reality of experience. What the Father and Son made objective and possible to all, the Spirit makes subjective and actual to the believer.*

The Full Range of Redemption

That the eye may aid to a better appreciation of the reach of redemption, from eternity past to eternity future, through the gracious work of the Trinity, we re-tell this remarkable story, as follows:

IN THE PAST—
>   The Father chose us as *His Very Own.*
>   The Son purchased us with His blood.
>   The Spirit persuaded us to believe.

IN THE PRESENT—
>   The Father gives us the position of sons.
>   The Son reveals His intimate mind and will.
>   The Spirit seals us as assuredly *His Very Own.*

IN THE FUTURE—
>   The Father will receive us fully accepted in Him.
>   The Son will inherit us as *His Very Own.*
>   The Spirit will claim us in final possession.

---

* For the full scope of the Spirit's work in our salvation, all too little appreciated by His born-ones, the reader is referred to the author's treatment of the subject in *His Indwelling*, page 29ff.

4—The Apostle's Prayer for the Believer, 1:15-23

In accordance with the Apostle's custom in addressing the various churches, he calls to mind his faithfulness in prayer for them. But he does more. He does
what is characteristic solely of the three epistles addressed to the spiritual man—Ephesians, Philippians,
Colossians: he breathes into the record the tenor of his
prayer, thus constituting it a corporate part of the
teaching; thus also expressing his confidence in, and de-
pendence upon, the Spirit of God to make these truths
live in men's lives.

Note

This prayer contrasts with that of Chapter 3. Here
the burden of petition is Light; there it is Love. Here
it is Divine Power; there it is Divine Presence. The
progress from the one to the other marks the essential
flow of the epistle itself.

"WHEREFORE" (1:15). This prayer has the closest
connection with what precedes, corresponding, petition
by petition, to the revealed working of the Father, of
the Son, and of the Spirit in our redemption, fervently
desiring to transmute these from the realm of mere
doctrine to that of personal knowledge and its resultant
experience. To this end it finds its climax in pointing
us to the present-day exaltation of Christ in glory, constituted the Head, the source and secret of the Church's
position and power to live and walk as His Body.

THE KEY TO CHRISTIAN KNOWLEDGE (1:17) is
"revelation." The Scriptures for the most part consist
of knowledge inaccessible to man apart from revelation, either objective or subjective. Reaching back into
the past, in part prehistoric; anticipating the future and
revealing the beyond, neither of which can be known,
save to God; unveiling a present life of intimate rela-

tionship to the Unseen—this is knowledge ministered only by the Holy Spirit as the Spirit of "wisdom and revelation," the ministry which is His office work for this age (John 16:12-15).

THE CHANNEL OF CHRISTIAN KNOWLEDGE (1:18a) is an enlightened heart. Not *mind,* as in the Authorized Version, but *heart.* Nor yet the heart as the seat of the affections, but including the intellect and will as well —the inner man. The "eyes of the heart" are this inner man's organs of sight, and of insight. Until the Holy Spirit has wrought His regenerating work this faculty of sight, the power to know spiritual things, is wholly lacking. "But the natural man receiveth not the things of the Spirit of God: for they are foolishness unto him: neither can he know them, because they are spiritually discerned" (1 Cor. 2:14). With this faculty restored, the believer must have his heart's eyes continually "enlightened" for a growing knowledge of spiritual truth.

THE CONTENT OF CHRISTIAN KNOWLEDGE (1:18b, 19a) consists of an appreciation of the blessings and benefits accruing to the redeemed, benefits concerning which the average believer remains amazingly ignorant and unappreciative. They result from the work (1) of the Father, (2) of the Son, (3) of the Spirit. We are to "know":

(1) "The hope of His calling." It is a hope to be known by turning back with prayerful meditation to the Father's choosing of us as His own, recorded in verses 3-6. It is a hope to be realized, in part now, as we "walk worthily of the calling wherewith we are called" (Eph. 4:1); and in full then, when we stand transformed in His presence.

(2) "The riches of the glory of His inheritance in the saints." What a piling up of terms! They are all

necessary to convey to our spiritual senses the unspeakable preciousness, not merely of His inheritance, held in store for us; but the glory of it; then, too, the riches of its glory. We will know this glorious wealth, our hereditary right in Christ, as we turn back to the Son's purpose in our redemption, recorded in verses 7-12. In doing so note the very words: *riches* (7), *inheritance* (11), *glory* (12). We will realize these riches now, as a present privilege, in proportion as we appropriate the depths and heights of Ephesian truth; then the inheritance, in full and final possession, will prove the more precious.

(3) "The exceeding greatness of His power to usward who believe. " Again the words used mark the futile effort of language to convey an adequate conception of the divine mysteries. To know this surpassing power we turn back to the part of the Holy Spirit in our redemption, recorded in verses 13, 14; then we move forward with awe and reverence through the matchless truths of this epistle as the unfolding of the Spirit's power in our lives "who believe," a power that is realized as we apprehend our position and privilege "in Christ" through the Spirit, our union, life, and walk "in Christ" by the same Spirit.

THE GUARANTEE OF THESE BLESSINGS BEING EXPERIENCED BY BELIEVERS (1:19b-23). The Christian system is not a theory; rather, it is a proved reality. The guarantee of its marvelous proposals toward us is this: that the program has already been carried out in the person of Christ, and that the same power employed in His case is the power He is prepared to exercise in our case. It is "according to the working of His mighty power, which He wrought in (the case of) Christ." The Greek means "the *manifested* strength of His *indwelling* might."

This might was manifested in Christ's case in a two-fold way: 1—by His resurrection from the dead (20a) ; 2—by His exaltation to the Father's right hand (20b). How can the program of redemption fail with such power placed at its disposal?

But the guarantee goes infinitely further. It is this: that Christ has been lifted to a position of absolute, universal authority (21, 22a), and in that position has been constituted "the head over all things to the church which is His body" (22b, 23). In other words, this power is administered through His exalted person, from His exalted position, by means of a vital, intimate union set up between Him and His redeemed; thus the power flows from Him into us as the life, mind, and will of the head flow into, and are expressed by the body.

Comment

WANTED—ENLIGHTENED HEARTS THAT SEE AND KNOW. Christian truth needs to be *seen* to be lived. The only faculty for seeing it is the heart, the inner life regenerated and enlightened by the Spirit. The failure of secular training lies in the fact that it addresses itself almost wholly to the head. But "the heart hath reasons which the head knows nothing of." Again, as someone has said, "All noble thoughts spring from the heart."

God's Word contains a psychology altogether truer than modern science in its constant reference to "the heart." It conceives of man's life as highly organized, unified, centralized, controlled from within, from one center of our complex being, physical, moral, intellectual, spiritual. Given the fact that God in regeneration becomes the author of this inner life in man; that He follows this by His indwelling presence; thus to become

its controller and constant inspirer—in this we have
provision for a heart that sees and knows.

But more. He links this life to Himself, making it
utterly responsive to His mind and will, in the most
intimate union, a union described as *"His body, the
fulness of Him that filleth all in all."* In this union His
redeemed are made partakers not only of the life and
power but of the program and destiny of the Son. What
a wonderful story! How entrancing our part in it!

Head of the Church, Thy Body,
O Christ, the great Salvation!
　　Sweet to the saints
　　It is to think
Of all Thine Exaltation.
All power's to Thee committed—
All power, on Earth, in Heaven;
　　To Thee a Name
　　Of widest fame
Above all glory's given.

With Thee, believers, raised,
In Thee on High are seated;
　　All guilty once,
　　But cleared by Thee;
Redemption toil's completed.
And when Thou, Lord and Saviour,
Shalt come again in glory,
　　There, by Thy side,
　　Thy spotless bride
Shall crown the wondrous story.

At length—the final Kingdom!
No bound, no end possessing!
　　When Heaven and Earth,
　　God—all in all—
Shall fill with largest blessing.
All root of evil banished,
No breath of sin to wither;
　　On Earth—on High—
　　Naught else but joy,
And blissful peace for ever!—*Anonymous.*

CHAPTER II

THE MOST WONDERFUL BODY EVER FORMED

EPHESIANS 2

His Very Own! Such was our God's intent and goal in Creation, when, as the crown and climax of it all came the counsel of infinite wisdom and love: "Let us make man." How? "In our image, after our likeness" (Gen. 1:26). Man was God's own, answering to Him as nothing in all the created universe could answer.

But sin intruded to sever the vital bond, to cheat the Lord God of His own and defeat His high purposes in man. Wherefore He said, "I will make him anew" (cf. Jer. 18:4 concerning the potter and his vessel of clay). This is the wonderful story of Ephesians 2. It is the marvel of a New Creation, wrought by Him who was "the beginning of the creation of God," coming to earth as a New Man, the beginning of a new order.

The plan involved His taking upon Himself a body, "prepared" for Him for the purpose, "in the likeness of sinful flesh and for sin," that therein He might do the will of God as the Old Man had failed to do, as the "old man" (in us) descended from Adam was incapable of doing. He was born into the human race. In a human body He lived His life of unbroken obedience to, and fellowship with His Father. Then, with supreme purpose, He gave up His body, His blood, His life, that from it might spring another New Man, like

45

unto Him in image, in life, in likeness, to walk the earth in His stead, so united to Him the Glorified, that he should be to Him in all truth a "body," His body, carrying out the will of his exalted Head.

Such a plan undoes the divisive ravages of sin, not alone Godward, by reuniting man and God in the oneness of head and body, but also manward, by making all classes one "in Him," in the oneness of a body.
Outline

II. Our Standing as the Body of Christ. The Threefold Work of the Triune God, 2:1-22.

1. We are His Body, Quickened by the Grace of God, the Father, 2:1-10.

    a. Our state by nature (1-3).
        (1) Dead in trespasses and sins (1).
        (2) Walking according to the **World** (2a).
        (3) Controlled by the spirit of **Satan** (2b).
        (4) Dominated by the desires of the **Flesh** (3).
        (5) Causing us to be children of disobedience (2c) and children of wrath (3b).

    b. God's interposition of grace (4-7).
        (1) Prompted by His great love (4).
        (2) Quickened and raised us WITH Christ (past) (5, 6a).
        (3) Seated us in the Heavenlies IN Christ (present) (6b).
        (4) Purposing in the coming ages to show the riches of His grace in His kindness to us THROUGH Christ (future) (7).

    c. The origin and outcome of salvation (8-10).
        (1) Not of our own works; by grace, through faith. a gift (8, 9).

    (2) Unto His good works, chosen of God
        that we should walk in them (10). (Con-
        trast the "walk" of v. 2.)

2. We are His Body, Formed by the Blood of Christ, the Son, 2:11-17.

  a. What we **were** by nature (11, 12).

    (1) Gentiles, outside the pale of religious rec-
        ognition (11a).

    (2) Called uncircumcision by the circumci-
        sion in the flesh (11b).

    (3) As such, without Christ, without a place
        among God's people, without a share in
        His covenants, without hope, without
        God in the world (12).

  b. What we **are** in Christ Jesus (13-17).

    (1) Made "nigh" by the Blood of Christ
        (13).

    (2) Made "one" in Christ (14-17).

      (a) He **Is** our Peace (14, 15a).
          The two made "one"—the middle
          wall of partition broken down.

      (b) He **Made** Peace (15b, 16).

  Method—the two made "One New Man" in
  Himself.

  Result—the two reconciled to God in "one
  Body."

      (c) He **Preached** Peace (17).
          To both—the "far off" and the
          "nigh."

3. As the One Body—We Have Access by the One Spirit, 2:18.

Our Access is

a. Through the Son.

b. By the Spirit.

c. Unto the Father.

4. **Formed Thus into the One Body We Become also His Building, 2:19-22.**
   a. We are the Household of God (19).
      Once Foreigners, now Fellow-Citizens.
   b. We are a Temple in the Lord (20, 21).
      (1) Its Foundation—Apostles and Prophets (20a).
      (2) Its Corner Stone—Jesus Christ (20b).
      (3) In Him is its Unity and Growth (21).
   c. We are His Habitation through the Spirit (22).

Note—The Building, here introduced, becomes the theme of Chapter 3.

Chart. See opposite page.

Our Standing As His Body is (to be) visualized for us in this section. The lofty truth which Chapter I reached and revealed as its conclusion and climax, that Christ exalted is "head over all things to the Church, which is His body," is the theme unfolded in Chapter 2.

The Work of God, Son, Spirit constitutes both the threefold division of the chapter and its outstanding feature. This is the more striking as we consider in detail its correspondence with Chapter 1. Again the trinity of God is not a theory or doctrine, but a practical, working reality in redemption.

Emphasis Upon the Son. As in Chapter 1 the Father holds the prominent place in planning Redemption—all is the working out of that plan—so here the emphasis passes to the Son, in providing redemption. "Blood of Christ" is its center and core. By it the "Grace of God" is conveyed (1-10); by it the dire need of man is met (11-18).

The Reach of Redemption, not only spiritually

Ephesians — HIS VERY OWN

	STANDING			WALK-ING		WAR-ING
	CHAP. 1 AS HIS **BELIEVERS**	**CHAP. 2** AS HIS **BODY** 1:22-23	**CHAP. 3** AS HIS **BUILDING** 2:19-22	4:1-5:20	5:21-6:9	6:10-24
FATHER CHOSE / ADOPTS WILL / ACCEPT 1:3-6		QUICKENED BY THE GRACE OF GOD 2:1-10				
SON PURCHASED ENLIGHTENS WILL INHERIT 1:7-12		MADE ONE BY THE BLOOD OF CHRIST 2:11-17				
SPIRIT SAVED SEALS WILL CLAIM 1:13,14		ACCESS BY THE ONE SPIRIT 2:18				
Prayer/Revelation Power/Resurrection	HE-Our Peace WE-Fellowcitizens	AMEN		BRIDE-TO BE		AMEN

IN HIM— *Our Standing in Heaven*   IN US— *His Walking on Earth*

49

but racially, is succinctly suggested in the concluding space. He is our Peace, uniting all classes in one life, one family, one citizenship. Other than his blood-purchased peace there is no solution of this world-wide problem.

Our Standing as the Body of Christ

It is of utmost importance that we get clearly in mind the transitional connection between Chapter 1 and Chapter 2. The key to the connection is the word "dead" (2:1), a state in which Jesus Christ our Lord became one with us. His life story is that He, in the body, (1) became dead; (2) was quickened from the dead; (3) was caused to sit in the heavenlies—1:20, 21. So we: (1) were dead; (2) as His body we were quickened from the dead; (3) made to sit in the heavenlies in Him—2:1-6.

1—Quickened by the Grace of God, the Father,
2:1-10

Note

WHAT WE WERE (2:1-3). Before we can appreciate what God undertook to do for us in grace, we must see ourselves, wholly undone, apart from His interposition. This is the logical course pursued everywhere in God's Word. It is a course rendered absolutely needful by the deceitfulness of the human heart, whereby man would deny his sinfulness. Such denial is seen on all sides today. The natural mind of man acknowledges no need of salvation. Hence we find God's treatise on salvation, the Epistle to the Romans, adopting a line of reasoning that displays: first, man's need; second, God's method of meeting the need.

That our minds may be open to God's thought in this crucial matter we should turn for the moment to the Romans statement of the case:

(1) WHAT MAN IS AND DOES BY NATURE (Rom. 1:18-3:20). It is the most searching, thoroughgoing and conclusive arraignment of the human race to be found in all literature. It condemns man's sinfulness, laying a sure foundation for his rightful conviction, upon a twofold count: that man forsook the glory of God—the root nature of all sin; that man has corrupted his ways—the inevitable fruit from the root.

(2) WHAT GOD HAS DONE IN CHRIST (Rom. 3:21-5:21). It is the story of matchless *grace* whereby He passed the judgment He has proved us deserving of, this "worthy of death" judgment, upon His own Son, that we might be justified from it by His *blood*, not by any merit on our part, for He has shown us possessed of none, either by nature or conduct, but rather by a *faith* in Him that appropriates His righteousness and life.

The italicized words are the very ones that stand out in the story of Ephesians 2, showing the second half of the two pictures to be the same. But this is equally true of the first half, and it is with this that we must first concern ourselves. We must ponder it well in its delineation of what we are:

(1) DEAD IN SINS (2:1). It is a sad, but truthful picture of the state into which we have come "through trespasses and sins," such trespasses and such sins as are common to the race. We are not being charged with any particular trespasses or sins, but rather with the state into which they, in an unbroken inheritance from Adam down, have brought us. That state is death. We are sundered from God; our life-cord is severed. Death is a state of unresponsiveness, as to both sensation and motion; therefore He can do

nothing to satisfy us and we can do nothing to satisfy Him. In such a case we were necessarily

(2) Disobedient to God (2:2, 3a). When sin took us out of the life of God it took us also out of the service of God. When we separated ourselves from God we sold ourselves to other masters, to obey whom is to disobey Him. Faithfully does Scripture here, as elsewhere, warn us of the threefold system of sin's enslavement: 1—The World, for we "walked according to the course of this world." We went the way of the world because our nature was responsive to its desires and aims as not to God. 2—Satan, for we walked "according to the prince of the power of the air." This phrase is a remarkable acknowledgment by Scripture of Satan's power in the higher reaches of the air, supplemented by the statement that this same one is "the spirit that now worketh in the children of disobedience," causing us to be characterized, as this orientalism conveys, by disobedience as our nature and birthright. 3—The Flesh, for "we all had our manner of life in times past in the lusts of our flesh, fulfilling the desires of the flesh and of the mind." What a portrayal of human life, controlled by a sin-prompted and sin-responsive nature, making answer to its degraded "lusts" and degrading "desires."

(3) Deserving of Wrath (2:3b). Here we meet the same Hebraism as above. To illustrate its use we turn to Deut. 25:2, where the original reads "son of strokes" and is translated "worthy to be beaten." Dead in sins—disobedient to God—deserving of wrath: what a diagnosis of man's moral and spiritual disability; and it comprehends us "all" for the simple reason that we are thus, not merely because of what we have done, which might include only the worst of sinners, but "by nature," which puts us all under a common condemna-

tion. Moreover, if there is to be a remedy, it must go deeper than conduct, or even character; it must set life right at the source.

WHAT GOD DID (2:4-9). If a wise and just God attempts an answer to human need, it is certain to be sufficient. And it is—the marvel of angels and men.

"BUT GOD" (4a). These two words mark the turning point of human destiny. Man could not help himself; left to his own resources he must perish. *But God* —God intervened, turning death into life, despair into hope, and that hope realized.

What He *did* is but the expression of what He *is*. He is here depicted as "God who is rich"; His riches, His resources, are in Himself. Out of the riches of His own nature flows the remedy for the need existing in our nature.

THREE GREAT WORDS are used to trace this matchless remedy to its source in God the Father:

(1) MERCY (4b). Mercy is our first need. If a man who deserves punishment is to escape it must be through the extension of mercy. In this quality God is "rich." The Scriptures abound in allusions to His mercy. We cite one familiar passage in the hope that it may become doubly precious in this setting:

"The Lord is merciful and gracious, slow to anger, and plenteous in mercy. He will not always chide: neither will He keep His anger for ever. He hath not dealt with us after our sins; nor rewarded us according to our iniquities. For as the heaven is high above the earth, so great is His mercy toward them that fear Him. As far as the east is from the west, so far hath He removed our transgressions from us. Like as a father pitieth his children, so the Lord pitieth them that fear Him. For He knoweth our frame; He remembereth that we are dust. As for man, his days are as grass: as a flower of the field, so he flourisheth. For the wind passeth over it, and it is gone; and the place thereof shall know it no more. But the mercy of the Lord is from everlasting to everlasting upon them that fear Him, and His righteousness unto children's children; to such as keep

His covenant, and to those that remember His commandments to do them"
(Ps. 103:8-18).

Mercy glories against judgment in that it rejoices to pardon, provided a way can be found in keeping with justice. And "Love found the way."

(2) Love (4c, 5a). Here we are again thrown back upon the nature of God, for "God *is* love"—and out of that inexhaustible nature He loved us "even when we were dead in sins." The fact that our hopeless, unlovely condition failed to deter His redeeming love— this fact proclaims His love supremely "great."

Love has the two elements, *desire* and *delight*. The one is the essence of His love toward us as sinners; the other, His love for us as saints, when we have become *His Very Own*. The one had the other in view. The latter love seems somewhat comprehensible to us; but the former—that He desired us when *dead*—how amazing! In contrast to all human love, we read: "But *God* commendeth His love toward us, in that, while we were yet sinners, Christ died for us" (Rom. 5:8).

(3) Grace (2:5b). Grace is God's undeserved favor. As a principle of dealing with men it is antithetical to law. Law does two things: 1—It demands a certain standard of conduct, in conformity to God's righteous requirement of man; 2—It condemns man in view of His inability and failure to keep its requirements. Grace, on the other hand, meets the needs of the case by doing two things: 1—It provides the righteousness which God's righteousness rightfully requires under law, setting that righteousness to our account as though it were our own; 2—On the basis of this provided righteousness it sets aside man's demerit and illdesert, as though it were not, that it may bestow upon him what he does not merit—God's undeserved favor.

The purport of the picture in Eph. 2:1-3 is to enforce the fact that "by grace ye are saved," as the only possible way. We were dead in sins, disobedient to God, deserving of wrath; our inability, our ill-conduct, our ill-desert—these leave us in darkness and despair, helpless and hopeless. *But God has wholly reversed the situation, by His mercy, His love, His grace.* All these, as the sole source and secret of salvation, together with the "kindness" of vs. 7, are comprehended in the Old Testament's magnificent phrasing, "lovingkindness and tender mercies."

Three Great Results are now to claim out attention as the accomplishment of grace in the benefits accruing to us. They are of a past, present and future character. They, too, are conveyed to us by three small words, the prepositions *with, in, through.*

(1) With Christ we *were* raised from the dead (2:5, 6a). This is a past-tense, finished and completed fact. This took place, in the intent of His grace, at, with, and through the resurrection of His own Son. To appreciate this teaching we must turn again to Romans 6. We deserved death. He for our sakes counted His own Son worthy of death. Judicially He died our death, and we died with Him. Likewise His resurrection. It was not merely His, but ours; we were raised with Him. What an escape from our sinful, condemned estate! What also are the moral implications, the spiritual results, of a with-Christ death to sin and life to God! Read and ponder Rom. 6:8-13; Col. 2:20-3:4.

(2) In Christ we are *now* seated in the Heavenlies (6b). This is a present-tense fact, glorious in achievement, abounding in assurance, decisive in victory. It touches the very heights of the most lofty Ephesian

truth. The basis of such a statement, so wholly inexplicable to the unregenerate mind, to the one who has no conception of our standing in Christ—its basis is the Body of Christ, His mystical Body, answering to His personal body, so vitally united to Him that what is true of the Head is true of the Body. He died; He rose; He ascended; He is seated at the Father's right hand. But we are "in Him"; and in Him we too, not representatively but actually, are seated there. What a contrast from that which we were. Marvellous change! What shall we say of a salvation achieving such a result?

(3) THROUGH CHRIST He *is going to* display "the exceeding riches of His grace in His kindness toward us" (2:7). This is a future-tense benefit, as certain as anything He has done or is doing. Here is His purpose, the fixed goal of it all, "in the ages to come," which so much Christian teaching totally ignores. In the day of His manifestation in power and glory— then it is that the Father is going to display through Christ the inexhaustible riches and the unlimited reach of His kindness toward us. What a display it will be! The principalities and powers, angelic and demoniac, will see it and know that God has triumphed, not in His wrath but in His kindness. And it is kindness toward us, His redeemed, *His Very Own* for eternity.

SALVATION'S ORIGIN AND OUTCOME (2:8-10). These verses serve as a conclusive deduction from all that precedes as to the certainty, source, and sufficiency of salvation.

SALVATION IS CERTAIN: "Ye *are* saved" (2:8). Assuredly. How can one read what God has done to this end and for a single moment call into question the certainty of the result. Ours is not a fate left to fortuitous circumstances. "Ye are saved." No enemy of God

will ever taunt Him with untruthfulness by producing
evidence that this one statement of His Word is in any
wise false. *"Ye are saved."*

NOT OF OURSELVES, BUT OF GOD (2:8, 9). Whence
came it? From God, of course. But, what of man's
part? "By grace—through faith." The grace is God's,
the faith is ours; so we are partners. But not so, as
some would have it. "Not of yourselves: the gift of
God." (The words "it is" are not in the Greek.) The
grace that gave the Saviour gives also the faith to appropriate Him. Otherwise man would credit himself
with his faith as an act of merit. But no; "Not of
works, lest any man should boast." God will leave no
room for this. If man is to be saved, it must be wholly
of grace that all boasting may be excluded. These two
statements sum up what precedes. Man has *nothing*
to his credit: necessarily, after verses 1-3. God has
done *everything:* truly so, in the light of verses 4-7.

WHAT WE HAVE BECOME (2:10). This is the cli-
mactic conclusion of what He has done, not we, stated
in terms of the change wrought and the responsiveness
secured in our own personal lives. This outcome, explicitly and of purpose, brings to light a threefold contrast with what we were:

(1) A NEW CREATION. The Christian system is
nothing short of this. We are "created"; not educated,
trained, cultured, into something better. Those who
substitute education for regeneration do the cause of
Christ and those whom they profess to help an irreparable injury. The product of their effort is not Christian, nor is it accepted of God: "Except a man be born
again, he cannot see the Kingdom of God." Men must
be "created in Christ Jesus" by the provision and opera-
tion of God's grace. The first creation, in Adam, be-

came dead in sin (Eph. 2:1). To meet the case, God took up His creative work again; He made it anew and gave it life. "If any man be in Christ, he is a new creation" (2 Cor. 5:17, R.V.).

(2) His Workmanship. That which He has wrought creatively, in His own likeness, is alive toward Him, reflects His mind, responds to His will—such we now are. The Greek for "workmanship" is *poema,* transliterated as our word "poem." That is to say, we are the highest, finest, most beautiful expression of His thought, His master-piece, that upon which He has bestowed His best, therefore surpassing His first creation. How wonderful! The first defected from Him, became disobedient to Him, stamped with the world, the flesh, and the devil (2:2, 3a). He made it anew, with the impress of His divine creatorship, so intimately *His Very Own* that none can mistake the fact.

(3) Good Works now occupy us. They are works of a particular sort; works prepared beforehand by Him, in anticipation of our restored ability and readiness to engage in them. They are, therefore, works that please Him and bind us to Him. Heretofore we were both disobedient and deserving of wrath (3b). Now, thanks to the triumph of grace, we are found walking in His chosen ways, responsive to His will, enjoying His approbation. We are, in living reality, *His Very Own.*

Not "Of" but "Unto" (2:9, 10). God will leave no room for mistaking the source and nature of our salvation. We of this picture, spiritually dead, had no works to offer. God did the working, and salvation is wholly of Him, "the gift of God" (Rom. 6:23). It is "not of works"; but it is "unto good works." It must never terminate upon ourselves. Failing to issue in these God-prepared works it misses its purpose.

Comment

SCIENCE SUBSTANTIATES SCRIPTURE. False teachers, who refuse to acquiesce in Christ's pronouncement of man's absolute need of the New Birth not only run counter to ordinary experience and observation—any one with his eyes open knows that human nature is radically wrong—but today they find science setting them down as unscientific. For example, at the First International Congress on Mental Hygiene, held at Washington, D. C., May, 1930, Dr. Frans Alexander, a psychoanalyst of Berlin, declared that, contrary to the popular conception that it is natural to be a law-abiding citizen, mental science has shown that people are born criminals and that all children, if they were free to respond to their instinctive impulses, would act as criminals. Other scientists speak similarly. This being true, in a picture, such as we have been examining, Scripture has given us a scientific diagnosis of man's need and a scientific remedy therefor.

SIN-MARRED MATERIAL FOR HIS BODY. Such is the significance of the opening description of this chapter. When God first would fashion a body for man, He used the dust of earth. When now He would form a body for His Son, for Himself, for His glory, He must needs use what sin had marred and scarred. This He did, pouring His life into it, graciously reviving it, and the resulting work of His grace and power is to us the more wonderful.

SITTING AND WALKING. That it is a real body He is fashioning is already evident from these attributed postures, "sitting" (6) and "walking" (10). Yet it has a reach that makes it the most wonderful body ever formed. Its sitting is in the Heavenlies, in Christ its glorified Head, whereas its walking is here upon the earth. It is through our walk that He is made manifest. He is seen in us.

HIS POEM. How sacred life becomes when we see ourselves snatched from a state of dead unresponsiveness and quickened by His creative touch into a life capable of registering and reflecting His most lofty thought and most loving purpose. With no good works to our credit at the outset, what wonderful possibilities lure us on. Day after day, line upon line, the poem moves on toward the perfect expression of His mind and heart and will. A wealth of good works, *pre*prepared, lures us on to the most worth-while life imaginable—fitting into the unfolding of a marvelous life-plan, fresh, day by day, moment by moment, from the hand of the Master Planner of lives.

2—Formed by the Blood of Christ, the Son, 2:11-17

Note

Up to this point we have had in view the individual, whether as sinner or as believer. Now we pass to the collective, and find the two divisions of the race, Jew and Gentile, brought before us. Not that the blood of Christ lacks efficacy for the individual, but that it goes immeasurably beyond the individual's needs and avails to remove the barriers of race and class.

It is absolutely vital to our grasping of the lofty message of unity and oneness in Ephesians that we see clearly and weigh fully this transition from the individual to the corporate. Our need of salvation goes deeper than the individual, even to the corporate state of society, seeing He "hath made of one blood all nations of men." This solidarity of the race is a solidarity in sin, out of which an individual cannot rise and separate himself. But salvation fully meets this situation. It provides new "blood" as the basis for a new solidarity; it sets up a new society "in Christ." We are saved, it is true, individually; but we do not live the saved life individually, for we are immediately baptized as units into an organism. Here, in Him, we partake of a common life. This enables Him to unify and harmonize human life in Himself. He is Himself, incorporated into our life, the only eradicator of human hatreds.

WHAT WE WERE IN OURSELVES (2:11, 12). We are called upon to "remember" what we were "in time past"—thanks to God's grace it is "past"—that "at that time," namely, before Christ came in the fullness of God's time to intervene, we were in a state of hopelessness.

The hopelessness, as here stated, is not that of our moral condition, sunk in personal sin. This was brought to our mind in verses 1-3. But now, in addition to being morally and individually undone, we were dispensationally and collectively in the same plight. The elements of our situation were these:

(1) We were "Gentiles in the flesh" (11a). We belonged to the great unsaved mass of humanity that, issuing from the purifying waters of the flood, went out over the face of the earth to corrupt themselves with all manner of idolatries and immoralities. Whether as wandering tribes or as great nations, their history down through the centuries is that they lived their lives and died "in the flesh." How and why this was so is graphically depicted in Romans 1:18-32. It is a state of inexcusableness, since they knew God from the

beginning (vv. 18-20). But—"When they knew God, they glorified Him not as God, neither were thankful" (vs. 21). The effect of leaving the living God out of their lives was a falling away into folly and idolatry (vv. 21-23), followed by awful and unspeakable moral and spiritual degradation (vv. 24-32). In this same state God sees the Gentile world still, condemned, "in the flesh."

(2) We were "called Uncircumcision by that which is called Circumcision in the flesh made by hands" (11b). It was thus that the Jews contemptuously styled the Gentiles, "Uncircumcision." They regarded them as entirely outside the pale of religion, without rights or standing. Spiritually they were to them as "dogs." (In testing the Syro-Phoenician woman's faith our Lord Jesus reminded her of this, using the same epithet; the woman humbly accepted it and turned it to her profit—Matt. 15:22-28.)

But Paul uses a phrase that lowers the Jew to much the same level. While they were "Gentiles in the flesh," the Jew deserves to be called "Circumcision in the flesh." Paul terms it "concision," a mere cutting in the flesh that has lost its spiritual import of an incision circumscribed about the heart to effect a separation unto God. This Jewish formalism, leaving the heart unchanged, adds infinitely to the problem. It is the secret of racial bigotry and race hatred, untouched by God's love. It rejected the Messiah. It refused to regard a Gentile as "brother" or share with him its privileges.

(3) We were "without—" (12). In every particular, especially as here enumerated, we were *without*: not only because we had gone away from God, but also because those who professed to know Him would not reach out a hand to bring us back to Him. (When

they refused God graciously turned their unbelief to our advantage, for we read: "Through their fall salvation is come to the Gentiles.")

Consider your hopelessness under the five counts. We were: 1—Without Christ, who belonged to Israel, associated with them even in preincarnation experiences (1 Cor. 10:4), until the Cross made Him a world Saviour; 2—Without a place among God's people, alienated from the citizenship, the corporate life, which Israel enjoyed with God as Lawgiver and King; 3—Without a share in His covenants, not one but many, repeated and reiterated, preëminently "covenants of promise," in which He pledged Himself to them; 4—Without hope—a statement saturated with significance when we consider that the Gentile world at the coming of Christ had sunk into a moral hopelessness, apparently beyond recovery; 5—Without God in the world, having gods many, none of which could help them, but no God—out *in the world* which sin and degradation had ruined.

WHAT WE ARE IN CHRIST (2:13-17). This is presented in the sharpest possible contrast, no feature of which should be overlooked: 1—"In time past," "at that time"—"But now"; 2—"We were"—"we are"; 3—What we were in ourselves—what we are "in Christ"; 4—"Far off"—"Nigh."

"BUT"—"BUT" (2:4, 13). Together these tell the whole story. The first is God's answer to our personal, individual need; the second is His answer to our dispensational, racial need. The two supplement each other, making a complete and wholly sufficient remedy for human ill.

WE ARE "MADE NIGH BY THE BLOOD OF CHRIST" (2:13). All that formerly left us "far off" is now re-

moved. There is no barrier to our near approach, with
all confidence. We have every right that any one could
possibly have. This is so because we are *now* "in
Christ." It is not that we personally have been changed.
Far more; our position is changed. We "are made
nigh." And there is just one means that could effect
this—"by the blood of Christ."

Atonement is the scarlet thread along which the
eternal purpose of God travels throughout Scripture.
Solemnly has He declared: "Without shedding of
blood is no remission." This statement He has enforced
by the entire ceremonial law and sacrificial system. But
now to this negative ministry of the Blood, if we may
so refer to the removal of our sin and disability, is
added the positive ministry here set forth: by the Blood
of Christ, shed for us, we have become *His Very Own,*
blood-bought, blood-related to God and to all, Jew and
Gentile, in Christ. How wonderful this is! We are
not merely made nigh. Listen!

WE ARE "MADE ONE" IN CHRIST (2:14-17). Doubtless this is the reason why the word *atonement* practically disappears in the New Testament. By the Blood
of the New Covenant not only is our sin "covered"
(the root meaning of atonement), but we are personally incorporated into His person, made a part of Himself. Thus most evidently is peace secured not only
between man and God but between every divergent
element of humanity, since all who believe on Him are
"in Him."

This story of peace is told as a threefold achievement:

(1) He *Is* Our Peace (14, 15a). The word *peace* is
doubtless employed as a reference to the "peace-offering." The prescription for the peace-offering is that it
should be "without blemish," setting forth the sinless-
ness of His person (Lev. 3:1) ; also, "an offering made

by fire unto the Lord," picturing the wrath due for sin which He received in our stead (Lev. 3:3).

Peace results for "both," in that He "hath broken down the middle wall of partition," referring to the Temple's outer court for the Gentiles, separated from the inner court into which only Jews might enter. But now, "Christ is the end of the law for righteousness to every one that believeth" (Rom. 10:4). Therefore He has "abolished in His flesh the enmity, even the law of commandments, contained in ordinances." Those who have them are not accepted for keeping them; those who have them not are no longer debarred through not keeping them: Christ alone is the basis of acceptance. He is indeed our peace: nothing and no one else.

(2) He *Made* Peace (15b, 16). The peace that He made—and here we reach the heart of the whole story —is described as to its unique *method* and its unique *result.*

The method of the divine wisdom and plan was to "make in Himself of twain one new man." This is God's carefully considered solution for the problem of sin, not only individual but corporate. It is not to patch up the old creation, educating and training human nature to behave better and treat one another with less of enmity and more of love. This is man's wisdom. But God's wisdom is to take any Jew and any Gentile, or any number of either, and of them make "one new man." Not an improving of the old creation; no, this is an absolutely "new creation" (2 Cor. 5:17).

The result is a oneness neither outward nor mechanical, but inward and vital. In this new creation both are reconciled to God "in one body." It is a new start, with former divisions and differences laid aside. Reconciled to God; the separation of sin out of the way;

partakers of His life and nature; responsive to His mind and will as His *body;* harmonized each with the other, in loving accord, as members of the *one* body— what a solution!

And the means to this marvelous end? He effected it "by the cross." There He gave His body in sacrifice, that from its poured-out life He might form a new body. There He suffered "in His flesh," the perfect meeting-ground of God and man, that He might reconcile to God every race and condition of men. There, slain by the enmity of men, He has in turn "slain the enmity" that existed between God and man and men and men. Thank God for the making of such peace!

(3) He *Preached* Peace (17). When peace has been made it must be made known. In His coming to earth the angels made the first Gospel pronouncement: "Good tidings of great joy . . . a Saviour . . . peace" (Luke 2:10, 11, 14). Having accomplished redemption He came anew in the person of His Spirit (John 14:16-18), empowering His followers to proclaim to all, Gentiles and Jews, this message of peace. Today, in His one Body, He is going to the ends of the earth, enabling men to "preach the gospel of peace, and bring glad tidings of good things" (Rom. 10:15).
Comment

THE PROBLEM OF PEACE is age-long and in our day has reached an acute stage. War and strife cover the pages of human history. Men have wearied of it. Moreover, modern science has made war a dangerous, desolating occupation. It now threatens extermination to those who indulge in it. Hence the herculean efforts to effect peace pacts. But they are all necessarily doomed to end in disappointment: "For when they shall say, Peace and safety; then sudden destruction cometh upon them, as travail upon a woman with child; and they shall not escape" (1 Thess. 5:3).

The inevitableness of the failure is in this brief but tremendously significant section of Scripture now before us. If God, as the moral governor of the universe, having made peace by means of the Cross, a method that represents the wisdom of eternity and that confessedly cost Him beyond all compute, were now to permit men who spurn and set aside His peace provision to come together under the stress of their circumstances and effect a peace of their own that would prove permanent—what would it be but a confession on God's part that He had changed His mind regarding His Son; that His method of the Cross was a failure; that man's wisdom was better than His. No! God could never so betray His Son. His peace is the one hope of world peace.

THE PERSON AND WORK OF CHRIST are central to the whole Christian scheme. He *is* our peace, and He *made* peace. These two phases, one dependent upon the other, tell the story. The "teachings of Jesus" utterly fall, apart from His person and work. Could an angel or a mere man have taught everything Jesus taught, the Christian system would have by no means resulted. Had it been possible for Jesus to teach all that He did and yet be less than sinless there would be no basis for saving faith or changed life. The Blood is of the essence of God's requirement, and that blood must pertain to a sinless person, "as of a lamb without blemish and without spot."

The reason for this is in the very nature of God. As holy God, separate from sin, He must govern in accordance with His holiness. Sin has set up an impassable gulf between Him in His holiness and man in his sinfulness. There must be not only reconciliation but a basis for it. "The very safety and stability of the moral universe require that the character of the Sin-Forgiver should not degenerate into that of the sin-indulger, otherwise the very foundations would be removed, and light and darkness, sin and righteousness, heaven and hell, God and Satan, be (as in the heathen world they are) inextricably blended together. If the stream of mercy flow at all, it must flow from beneath the altar of justice" (William Graham).

It is characteristic of the Epistles, as a progression from the Gospels, that they lay hold of the person and work of Christ as making possible not only a reconciliation to God but a life of utter oneness with Him. The Blood that flowed so freely for us from His precious body, that blood has sufficed to form a *new body* into which we have been incorporated, to be made a part of His own person.

The New Man—this is the supreme triumph of grace. Not the old made over, but an entirely new entity, made up of any Jew and any Gentile who will, by faith in Christ, let God usher them into His new creation, "Where there is neither Greek, nor Jew, circumcision nor uncircumcision, Barbarian, Scythian, bond nor free: but Christ is all, and in all" (Col. 3:11), which is but a description of "the new man, which is renewed in knowledge after the image of Him that created him" (vs. 10). As the first creation was in His image, so now God remedies its marring by a remaking in that same image. How wonderful!

This is the very essence, the heart, the secret of the Christian system. Few pause to marvel at the wisdom of God's solution to the problem. The believer is not a *better* man, but a different; he belongs to another order, to another creation. God has made of all believers a new personality, of which each is a part, formed from His blood, born of His Spirit, springing from His person, yet vitally attached to His person, never living apart from Him but always as a part of Him—what a provision for the elimination not alone of enmity against God but of all possible race prejudice, personal animosity, pride of position or possession, or of class distinction! This New Man in Christ is the only solution, and it really solves.

ILLUSTRATION. From the world-wide field of applied Christianity a multiplicity of illustrations could be gathered. Dr. Frank A. Keller, of the Hunan Bible Institute, narrates the case of a barber, a class held in particplar contempt in China, and a student. The barber had become degenerate, addicted to opium and otherwise degraded. He had lost hope and turned to the Christian mission in the community as a last resort. A personal interest was taken in him. Prayer was answered; his heart opened to Christ; his appetite for opium instantly left; he became a living witness to the power of the Gospel. Meanwhile a man of the student class had sought the mission as an inquirer. Seeing the barber he refused to enter. Day after day he watched for the barber to depart before he would come in. One day, thinking the barber had left, he inadvertently met him. Too courteous to be rude, he suffered himself to enter into conversation. The barber was soon telling of the change Christ had wrought. Class barriers were rapidly melting away. Ere long the barber found himself a guest at the student's home, in surroundings of culture and wealth. Christ had indeed "made both one."

3—Access by the One Spirit, 2:18

The work of the Holy Spirit with reference to this New Man, while not wanting in the formation of the one Body, involving New Birth by the Spirit, is now specifically stated as an advance step, yet with utmost brevity—one short sentence—due to the fact that the Spirit's particular office in Ephesian truth awaits emphasis in Chapter 3.

Note

BOTH HAVE ACCESS. All advantage of the one or disadvantage of the other is lost in the common standing of both in the one Body in Christ. No other consideration counts; both are as one in Him. To this one New Man is given access, approach, audience, into the very presence chamber of the King.

This access involves the three persons of the Godhead, so that again we meet the Trinity, not as a doctrine but as a practical experience. Our approach is

THROUGH THE SON. He is the mediator of the New Covenant. It was He who "once suffered for sins, the just for the unjust, that He might bring us to God" (1 Pet. 3:18). It was He who declared: "No man cometh unto the Father but by Me" (John 14:6). In the Greek it is the same word as here in Ephesians—"through Me." Whether pouring out His life-blood on Calvary, or presenting this blood as the basis of His advocacy with the Father, it is always and only *through* Him that we come.

BY THE SPIRIT. When redemption has been wrought out *for* us, it is the Spirit that works it *in* us; He then moves in to possess the product of His regenerating power; it is then His prerogative to present us as the fruit of His grace during this Pentecostal age, the New

Man, made possible by the Son's sacrificial blood, supplemented by the Spirit's wooing love. What joy He has in introducing this New Man at the Court of Heaven.

UNTO THE FATHER. It was in the Father's heart that the plan of redemption originated; from the Father the love and grace that gave the Son proceeded; now back to the Father comes the fruitage—a New Man on earth answering to the New Man already in Heaven. What exceeding joy is His over a new Man, akin to Himself, whom He can welcome into His immediate presence.

Comment

THE CROWNING PROOF OF CHRISTIANITY is not in its ethics, nor in its theology, nor yet in its good works, but in this: it has produced a New Man who is approved of God. It is an incomparable achievement. God is still just, holy, pure, separate from sin; yet He has on earth a Man, made up from the most diverse elements of society, high and low, rich and poor, honorable and debased, and that Man is wholly and unequivocally acceptable to Him. How amazing it is! And the wonder grows as we proceed, fully vindicating His method of Grace, in that it has accomplished what nothing else could.

NO OTHER MEDIATOR. The Holy Spirit, acting as Introducer at Court, presenting His New Man—does He crave of Peter the privilege of passing? No. Does He consult the saints for their approval? No. Does He invoke the Mother of Jesus? No. As there is but one Mediator, so "through *Him* we both have access." We are in the sovereign hands of God the Spirit; coming by Him our appeal is solely to "the name that is above every name."

"But this man, because he continueth ever, hath an unchangeable priesthood. Wherefore He is able also to save them to the uttermost that come unto God by Him, seeing He ever liveth to make intercession for them" (Heb. 7:24, 25).

"Seeing then that we have a great high priest, that is passed into the heavens, Jesus the Son of God, let us hold fast our profession. For we have not an high priest which cannot be touched with the feeling of our infirmities, but was in all points tempted like as we are, yet without sin. Let us therefore come boldly unto the throne of grace, that we may obtain mercy, and find grace to help in time of need" (Heb.4:14-16).

4—The One Body Becomes also His Building, 2:19-22

Note

BELIEVERS—BODY—BUILDING. This is the progress of teaching in Ephesians, in the unfolding of our standing in Christ. From individual believers we are formed, collectively into one Body. But this is not all. Here, of necessity, the figure changes in order to convey the fuller marvels of His redemptive plan—we are also His Building.

As the close of Chapter 1 introduced the theme of Chapter 2; so now, in these closing verses, we are introduced to the theme of Chapter 3. For this reason we need dwell upon them but briefly.

THE TRINITY is again introduced as the unfolding of Christian experience. The "household" into which believers have been born is God the Father's; the "temple" into which we have been built is the Lord the Son's; the "habitation" for which He has chosen us is God the Spirit's.

"No More" (2:19) continues the contrast between what we were and what we are, carrying it, with a "now therefore," to an almost unbelievable climax. Not merely is it true that we who "were far off are made nigh"; we find ourselves established in the counsels of the Godhead in a most intimate and satisfying relationship. From being "strangers and sojourners," mere wanderers on the face of the earth, we have become a *nation*, even the chosen nation of God's people, with full provision for *city* and *family* life. Still more: we are the headquarters for His *worship*, and He has actually chosen us as the place of His personal abiding *presence*.

We are: 1—God's Household (19b), the Father's family, the center of His love and life. We need to rub our eyes, so to speak, we who were outcasts, spiritually "dogs," to make sure that so great a change is actually so. 2—The Lord's Temple (20, 21). This temple has for its foundation "the apostles and prophets" (doubtless of the New as well as Old Testament), that is, the truth committed to them to teach concerning the one Foundation (1 Cor. 3:10, 11). For its chief corner stone "Jesus Christ Himself"; He is Himself that which holds together the otherwise divisive parts, binding them into one building. He is also its secret of symmetry and growth, thus to fit each "living stone" into its purposed place in a matchless building for His worship and praise. 3—The Spirit's Habitation (22). When the Son had returned to the Father's side, with the Blood of Calvary's victory, the Spirit was sent forth to earth, according to promise; and He came claiming believers as His age-long abiding place.

It is this marvelous fact that becomes the theme of Ephesians 3.

Comment

THE MOST SACRED SPOT ON EARTH—where and what is it? Not any far-famed shrine, however many devotees may resort thither. Not any costly cathedral, however imposing or commanding. No spot that many may choose and consecrate. No building that man may erect and dedicate. All of these are but man's effort to make sacred. Not one can claim the actual abiding presence of the living God. Rather, the spot supremely sacred is that which He has chosen as His abode, His worshipping temple. It is the believer's heart. To see this is to have one's life transformed; no longer secular, but wholly sacred; constrained to cry, with Paul: "No longer I that live, but Christ that liveth in me"; consecrated, not by any act of ours so much as by the superlative fact that the Spirit of the living Christ of God lives within.

Blood-bought, to become *His Very Own!* How can we keep from overflowing in grateful praise?

> "Near, so very near to God,
> Nearer I cannot be;
> For in the person of His Son
> I'm just as near as He.
>
> Dear, so very dear to God,
> Dearer I cannot be;
> For in the person of His Son
> I'm just as dear as He."

CHAPTER III

THE MOST WONDERFUL BUILDING EVER BUILT

Ephesians 3

Once again, in turning to a new chapter in Ephesians, we find that the closing thought of the preceding chapter has supplied the theme for what follows. We are no longer thinking in terms of the Body; now it is the Building.

The transition of thought is a natural one. The mystical Body of Christ, formed from His blood, is the New Man which God now has upon earth. This New Man is made up of Jews and Gentiles by the one principle of faith in Christ. Those thus gathered into this new personality henceforth constitute God's people. They are fellow-citizens of His commonwealth. Yes, but still more intimately they are His children. They make up His household. As a Father He must provide a place in which to house them. That place is to be His temple, the holy temple in the Lord that He made us to be; then into that temple He comes with His gracious abiding presence.

The progress of thought is also evident, conveyed by the change of imagery. It may be stated thus:

The Body is possessed of His Life and Nature.
The Building is possessed of His very Presence.

This progress is the necessary completion of the mutual relationship between Himself and us, as taught by our Lord under the imagery of the Vine and the Branch. It may be stated:

> Chapter 2—Position in Christ: Ye in Me.
> Chapter 3—Possession of Christ: I in You.

As the New Man of Chapter 2, we have access to Him; He delights to have us come into His presence. As the New Building of Chapter 3 He has access to us; He comes into our abiding place, making it His abode. Now we can sing:

> "And not alone the gift of life,
> But His own Self He gave me."

The correspondence between the Old Covenant temple and the New, and yet the contrast occasioned by the passage from the Old to the New—through these will the vital teaching of Ephesians 3 unfold to us.

Outline

III. Our Standing as God's Building—Partition Removed — Gentiles Coequals — Filled with His Presence, 3:1-21.

    1. Paul the Minister of this "Mystery," 3:1-13.

        a.   To Paul was committed the Dispensation of Grace (1, 2).

        b.   To Paul was revealed the Mystery of the Church (3-5).

        c.   The nature of this Mystery: "Gentiles Fellowheirs and of the Same Body" (6).

        d.   Paul called to preach among the Gentiles the Unsearchable Riches of Christ (7-12).

            (1) That to all on earth might be known the mystery hitherto hidden in God (9).

            (2) That to all in the heavenlies might be known by the Church the eternally purposed wisdom of God (10-12).

    e. Paul's attitude toward his sufferings in this ministry (13).

2. **Paul's Prayer in Dedication of the Temple that God's Presence May Fill His House, 3:14-21.**

    a. A prayer addressed to the Father (14, 15).

    b. Seeking the threefold "Fulness" of the Triune God (16-19).

      (1) Strengthened in the inner man by His **Spirit** (16).

      (2) A Temple—indwelt by **Christ** (17a)— "grounded and founded in love" (17b) —its dimensions expanding to the very love of Christ itself (18, 19a).

      (3) "Filled unto all the fulness of **God**" (19b).

    c. Final words of dedication (20, 21).

      (1) Dedicated to the Limitless One (20a).
        "Able to do exceeding abundantly above all that we ask or think"

      (2) Limited only by His freedom to work in us (20b).
        "According to the power that worketh in us"

      (3) To such His New Testament Temple is dedicated (21).
        "Unto Him be glory in the Church by Christ Jesus . . . Amen."

      Compare the end of the prayer dedicating the Old Testament Temple—2 Chron. 7:1-3.

Chart—See following page.

THE TRINITY is again in evidence, explicitly stated in the threefold designation of the Building; Household of GOD; Temple in the LORD; Habitation in the SPIRIT.

Ephesians — HIS VERY OWN

	STAND-ING		WALK-ING		WAR-ING
	CHAP. 1	CHAP. 2	CHAP. 3	4:1-5:20	5:21-6:9	6:10-24
	AS HIS **BELIEVERS**	AS HIS **BODY** 1:22-23	AS HIS **BUILDING** 2:19-22			
	FATHER { CHOSE, ADOPTS, WILL ACCEPT 1:3-6	QUICKENED BY THE GRACE OF **GOD** 2:1-10	HOUSEHOLD OF **GOD** 3:1-13 — MYSTERY OF THE AGES			
	SON { PURCHASED, ENLIGHTENS, WILL INHERIT 1:7-12	MADE ONE BY THE BLOOD OF **CHRIST** 2:11-17	TEMPLE IN THE **LORD** 3:6 — PARTITIONS REMOVED			
	SPIRIT { SAVED, SEALS, WILL CLAIM 1:13,14	ACCESS BY THE ONE **SPIRIT** 2:18	HABITATION IN THE **SPIRIT** 3:14-21 — FILLED WITH GLORY			
	Prayer for **R**evelation / **P**ower of **R**esurrection	HE–Our Peace / WE–Fellowcitizens	**A**ble Exceeding **A**bundantly Above all we ask AMEN		**B**RIDE– TO BE	AMEN

IN HIM– *Our Standing in Heaven*   IN US– *His Walking on Earth*

EMPHASIS UPON THE SPIRIT. While in Chapter 1 the work of the Father is outstanding; while Chapter 2 stresses the work of the Son; here in Chapter 3 emphasis is placed upon the work of the Spirit. The constitution of the Father's household; the changes in the Lord's temple—these but prepare for the dispensation of the Spirit, even His indwelling presence and power. A diagonal line across the three sections of the chart would trace and visualize this progressive emphasis.

HOUSEHOLD OF GOD relates itself to the ministry of Paul to the Gentiles and the unveiling of the "mystery" of Gentile and Jewish coequality in Church constituency.

TEMPLE IN THE LORD relates itself to the change wrought in the temple by the Son's redemptive work, as recorded in Chapter 2, whereby the existing partition was abolished. All barriers are blood-banished.

HABITATION IN THE SPIRIT relates itself to the prayer of Paul whereby the "Building" is presented to God in dedication and the Presence comes in with fullness of power and glory.

THE APPEAL is for a complete committal of life, thus possessed, to the Limitless One, that the glory may truly be His.

AMEN divides the Epistle, making the three chapters a finished treatise on our Standing, bidding us pause to enter into the reality of it before passing to our Walk and Warfare.

1—Paul the Minister of this "Mystery," 3:1-13

Note

Throughout this entire chapter Paul is looking upon himself as the appointed minister of the New-Covenant temple. We might well give to its contents the

twofold analysis: 1—Paul in Prison (3:1-13); 2—
Paul in Prayer (3:14-21). Such a designation brings
to light the true connection between the two portions
and the appropriateness of the Apostle's reference to
himself as in prison, beginning and closing the portrayal of his ministry.

The Lord's Prisoner for Their Sakes (3:1).
The dash after verse 1 (see R.V.) is a characteristic
break in the Apostle's flow of thought. The reference
to his imprisonment leads him to a matter of the greatest import, occupying the entire Chapter. (See the
opening words of Chapter 4 for a resumed reference
to his imprisonment.) He seems to say something to
this effect: "You Gentiles know that I received this
ministry on your behalf, to make you members in full
equality in the Body of Christ. For this I am in prison. Yet, far from having you faint because of my
bonds, rather I crown my labors on your behalf by
turning to prayer, presenting you to the Father for the
experiencing of His empowering presence by His indwelling Spirit." There is the further thought that,
thus endued, they are rendered less dependent upon the
Apostle's ministrations (cf. Phil. 2:12, 13).

The New House-Management (3:2). The Greek
word for *dispensation* has in it the word *house*. It
means "the law of the house," the mode of regulating
it, its management. It is our word *economy*, which we
further qualify as *domestic*. God has a new plan to
introduce in the making up and regulating of His
household. Paul says that to him was the "grace" given
of being the steward or manager of this newly constituted household.

By the Revelation of Christ (3:3). The Apostle
traces his ministry to its source in the appearing of the

Lord Jesus Christ to him on the Damacus road. He saw the Lord. Not only was he thereby converted, turned about, as his people, the Jews, will be one day; but therefrom he received his apostleship. (Read Galatians 1 in this connection.) More than that, at the same time he received his call to be "the Apostle to the Gentiles" (Acts 9:15, 16; Gal. 1:15, 16). Then, also, he apparently received his initial "understanding in the mystery of Christ" (3:4, R.V.), supplemented by subsequent revelations promised at the time (read Acts 26: 16, 17). Human wisdom never devised or stumbled onto the plan of house-management which was there revealed for His Church.

THE MYSTERY OF CHRIST (3:4, 5). The word *mystery*, occurring three times in this brief section, does not mean something mysterious; rather, that which is discoverable only by revelation and is therefore hidden until the appropriate and appointed time for revealing it. Of this meaning we here have a clear statement: "Which in other ages was not made known . . . as it is now revealed."

What is the "mystery of Christ"? Of the several mysteries revealed in the New Testament four may be said to be referable to Christ: 1—The Mystery of Christ Incarnate (1 Tim. 3:16); 2—The Mystery of the Church as His Body (which we are now studying); 3—The Mystery of Christ's Indwelling (Col. 1:27); 4 —The Mystery of the Church as the Bride of Christ (Eph. 5:32). These all were hidden in previous ages.

THE MYSTERY OF THE CHURCH (3:6). This Concerns the Gentiles' position in the Body of Christ. It is not that they would be saved; this fact was revealed to and through the Old Testament prophets, e.g., the quotations in Rom. 9:25, 26; 10:19, 20. They anticipated

the fact that the Gentiles would find a place of favor
with the Old Testament people and that by faith, e.g.,
Rom. 15:9, 10; Gal. 3:8, 9.

The mystery is the radical change wrought by the
creating of a new entity, the Church, and the placing
of the Gentiles as coequals in it. This tremendous in-
novation of plan was revealed to Paul and committed
to him as the distinctive responsibility of his ministry.

The import of this change of plan is conveyed by
three Greek words, whose force is largely lost in translation, each having the prefix *sun,* meaning equals,
partners, together; that is, on the same footing, neither
inferior or superior to the other. The statement is that
through the Gospel the Gentiles have become

> Co-heirs (of God).
> Co-members of the body (of Christ).
> Co-sharers of the promise (of the Spirit).

Again we are face to face with the Trinity, so characteristic of Ephesians, sharing in the glorious triumph
of the redemptive plan. What a change has come
about. Instead of a chosen people, through whom
blessings might be had by less favored peoples of earth,
now the blessing flows from the Head through the
Body, into which all, immediately that they have accepted it, are drawn into the New Man and, in turn,
become channels of the same grace to others.

The Apostle's Ministry (3:7-12). Entrusted with
this matchless mystery, his ministry is necessarily that
of devoting himself to the making up of God's New-
Covenant household in keeping with this revealed plan,
the building of His New-Covenant temple in accordance with these specifications. So he proceeds to picture his ministry as follows:

(1) ITS SOURCE (3:7). "Whereof I was made a minister, according to the gift of the grace of God given unto me by the effectual working of His power." Elsewhere, in defending his apostleship, he declares: "For I neither received it of man, neither was I taught it, but by the revelation of Jesus Christ" (Gal. 1:12). Here he traces it to its divine source as "the gift of grace" and "the working of power."

(2) ITS SPIRIT (3:8a). Far from being puffed up by so exalted a commission, in utter humility he adds: "Unto me, who am less than the least of all saints, is this grace given." Elsewhere he styles himself "the chief of sinners," magnifying the Lord's mercy in his salvation (1 Tim. 1:15, 16). Again, he calls himself "the least of the apostles, not meet to be called an apostle," in remembrance of his record as persecutor of the Church, rendering the grace that called him all the more amazing (1 Cor. 15:9). And now he coins a word to convey his humility of spirit—a comparative is coupled with a superlative: "Less than the least of all saints." To think, says he, that to such as I "is this grace given"; namely, the preaching of such a gospel!

(3) ITS CONTENT (3:8b). "That I should preach among the Gentiles," those who have come into such a wonderful inheritance, "the unsearchable riches of Christ." These riches of our Lord Jesus Christ are described in one word as "unsearchable"; that is, beyond tracing out, incalculable because not fully discoverable. What we know of them is a mere suggestion of what they really are. As we know them, they are:

1—The riches of His essential glory; coequal with the Father; creator of all things; recipient of the worship and honor due to deity. 2—The riches of His voluntary self-impoverishment for our sake: who, "though

He was rich, yet for your sakes He became poor, that ye through His poverty might be rich" (2 Cor. 8:9); the story of His humiliation (Phil. 2:5-8); His willingness, though the Creator, to become the creature, in incarnation. 3—The riches of His moral glory: manifested as a man among men; the perfection of His personal character, incomparable with others; the wisdom falling from His lips—"never man so spake"; the wonders of His works—"we never saw it on this wise"; the rectitude of His walk, never excusing Himself for any error of judgment, of purpose or deed—in all this an example that remains unsurpassed, yea, unapproached. 4—The riches of His death: achieving His purpose in coming "to give His life"—with its qualities of deity and perfect humanity—"a ransom for many." 5—The riches of His mediatorial glory: raised and glorified; a Man in heaven; His ceaseless intercession for us; His opening of access to the Father; His watch-care as the "Great Shepherd of the Sheep." 6—The riches of His presence among His people: with us "all the days"; in us in transforming power, to reproduce His own character and likeness; the power of endless life. 7—The riches of His return and reign: the claiming of His own; the crown of promised reward; the calling of His Bride to share His kingdom-rights; the heirship of the ages, worlds known and unknown, made His and ours.

Surely such riches were sufficient to occupy the Apostle, once he had glimpsed by revelation even the millionth part.

(4) ITS INTENT (3:9-12), the end ever in view, is twofold: 1—Toward all on earth; 2—Toward all in the heavenlies.

"To make all"—that is, of whatsoever class or con-

dition, since the terms of the Gospel open it to all—
"see what is the dispensation of the mystery which for
ages hath been hid in God who created all things"
(3:9, R.V.). With so wondrous a proposal, formerly
"hid in God," now entrusted to the gospel preacher,
his one duty is clear, namely, to bend every effort, sup-
plementing that of the Apostle, to the one end of
making men see it.

Paul has a God "who created all things." So have
we. Despite every search for evidence to the contrary,
a universe apart from the moving, creative power of
God, as the explanation of its origin and continuance,
remains unthinkable. Life and energy must have a
Source. This becomes the more necessary when the
evidence of design is written over them. Genesis 1,
with the name *God* occurring thirty-one times in thirty-
one verses, will always stand as the true statement of
the origin and orderly arrangement of the universe of
which we are a part.

Thus Paul has a gospel that reaches, not only outward to all men, but upward to the heights of the
heavenlies. There are "principalities and powers,"
good and bad, of which we were told that Christ is now
seated far above them all (1:21). They experienced
His power in creation; to them must "be made known"
His wisdom in redemption. This knowledge is to come
to them "through the Church," the embodiment of
God's redemptive wisdom for the solution of the age-
long problem of sin in all of its ramifications. Far
from being the foolishness of God, that which He is
accomplishing in and through the Church will yet be
evidenced as the "much variegated" wisdom of God,
suggesting a tapestry into which are woven the many

threads and colorings that make it a work of skill and beauty. Listen!

According to the Plan of the Ages (3:11; see R.V. margin). Such is the central position the Church occupies in the eternal counsels of God. In these days we find it needful to do city-planning. God from eternity made His age-plans, and He made them around the Church. Holy Scripture reveals a progressive unfolding of the plans, covering the time-segment occupied by human history, frequently drawing aside the curtain for a glimpse of ages to come. In this disclosure the "mystery" of the Church occupies the center of the stage. Yet the plans are more comprehensive than our ordinary thought of the Church. They are such as He "purposed in Christ Jesus our Lord."

How far-reaching are these purposes in Christ Jesus was brought to light by His redemptive triumph whereby already the Father "hath put all under His feet," that is, "all rule and authority, and power, and dominion, and every name that is named, not only in this world, but also in that which is to come"; and further, "gave Him to be head over all" (1:22). Whatever realms of authority or being may exist, Christ is their head and they are at His feet. But, mediating between the Head and the feet, as it were, is "the church, which is His body, the fulness of Him that filleth all in all" (1:22,23). It is just a glimpse of the place accorded to Christ and His Church in the planning of the ages.

"Boldness and Access with Confidence" (3:12). What a piling up of words to persuade us of the privileged position which we, erstwhile sinners, now occupy, since we find ourselves, as the Church, at the very center of the divine mind and will! Christ is the accepted Mediator. But more; we come not merely *through*

Him but *in* Him—"accepted *in* the Beloved," in complete identification.   We come in the faith that is emboldened by the confidence that such a relationship can never be denied.

Thus does the Apostle lead up to the exercise of this prayer privilege by himself on our behalf, as we shall see in a few moments.   But before turning to prayer he exhorts them that they, having now glimpsed the wondrousness of this ministry on their behalf, faint not because it has brought him into bonds; rather that they should find occasion to glory in them (13).   The results far outweigh the cost.   Nor do his bonds hinder him in his highest ministry—prayer.

Comment

THE SOURCE OF PREACHING.   We hear much today about "sources."   Paul knew but one Source, spelled with a capital S.   Value our libraries as we may, the biggest and best of them never could serve as a substitute for this one fountain and inspiration of all truth and of all true preaching.   He who spoke as One having authority instills that much-needed note into the ministry of the man who, Paul-like, enters into the secret chamber of revelation, there to glimpse His face and know His mind.   How greatly is this to be desired today!   Fed so long on the tasteless rehashing of human thought, how the people long for the sparkling water of life, fresh from the heart of Him who is the Source of all truth and life.

THE SPIRIT OF HUMILITY.   Among the utterances that let us into the Apostle's inner life none is more illuminating than the styling of himself as "less than the least."   We count him the chief apostle.   So he is.   But he would not have been had he rated himself as such. "Whosoever of you will be the chiefest, let him be the servant of all." Paul's humility kept him serving. He endured persecutions, perils, hardships almost beyond belief, because in his humility he counted himself deserving of nothing better. And how may we attain this spirit? By the constant realization of what we are in Christ, contrasted with what we were in ourselves.

THE WEALTH OF THE GOSPEL is so munificent, so bounteous, so princely in its proportions; so inexhaustible—witness the countless volumes written to interpret the person of Christ, His atoning work, some phase of His redemption—moreover, so thoroughly adapted to the meeting of the moral and spiritual impoverishment of our race; such that the Apostle characterizes it as "unsearchable riches." Being such, with no rival worthy of mention, how can one explain the modern phenomenon of pulpits, dedicated to its heralding, becoming occupied, week after week, with the puerilities and trash of passing thought? Well did a metropolitan newspaper, after listing the sermon themes announced in its columns for the previous Sunday, dealing with politics, crime, law and order, philosophy, literature, the latest book, travel, etc., all skilfully worded to catch the popular fancy, raise the question editorially, *"Why not preach Christ?"* Why should men come to church to hear what they can as well read in the magazines at home? The modern man has not lost his sense of values. He knows wealth when he sees it. Why not hold out to him the riches of Christ?

THE WISDOM OF GOD has been much questioned and traduced in the face of sin and human suffering. Yet God is wise, and His wisdom will one day not only be vindicated but become the admiration of every sentient being. That wisdom has chosen the Church as its channel of expression, so Saint Paul declares, and will find its full disclosure in the consummation not alone

of this age but of the ages to come. What now is
known only in part, even by the heavenly hosts, of the
glorious goal of God's matchless grace will then be
openly displayed as the exhibit of His manifold
wisdom.

It should be noted that each one of these three matchless chapters of Ephesians contains a significant allusion
to this forthcoming disclosure of divine wisdom, the
ultimate realization of His "one increasing purpose."
In Eph. 1:9-12 we read of "the mystery of His will,
according to His good pleasure which He hath purposed in Himself: that in the dispensation of the fullness of times He might gather in one all things in
Christ, both which are in heaven and which are on
earth: even in Him; in whom also we have obtained
an inheritance, being predestinated according to the
purpose of Him who worketh all things after the counsel of His own will: that we should be to the praise of
His glory." In Eph. 2:7 we read: "That in the ages
to come He might show the exceeding riches of His
grace in His kindness toward us through Christ Jesus."
And now in Eph. 3:10, 11: "To the intent that now
unto the principalities and powers in heavenly places
might be known by the church the manifold wisdom
of God, according to the eternal purpose which He
purposed in Christ Jesus our Lord."

What can it mean but that for the coming ages is
reserved a revelation of God's purposes in grace so far
beyond the present power of man to conceive, as will
make evident to all created intelligence the many-sided
wisdom of God in creation, and especially in redemption. Even sin, having occasioned His grace, will con-
tribute to the glory of that consummation. In that new

order the Lamb and His Bride will ever be central—
Wisdom embodied in Love.

The possible proportions of this triumph of wisdom
stagger the human mind. As all creation shared the
curse, just so, in the new heavens and new earth, all
creation shall be rejuvenated. But what is creation's
extent? Just seven years prior to this writing science
discovered worlds 110,000 light years away from the
earth, an almost inconceivable distance (light travelling
186,300 miles every second for 110,000 years). But today, having found "universes" 1,000,000 light years
away, they pass beyond that to tell us of other universes
140,000,000 light years from us. What this means is
incomprehensible, except by contrast. The contrast is
this: it takes but 8 minutes for light to travel to us from
our sun. Compute the ratio of 8 minutes to 140 million
years. To the finite mind space becomes infinite.
Think of the myriads of universes, with their lesser
bodies, contained therein. For them all grace turned
threatened chaos into effulgent glory.

Moreover, it is purposed, and promised, that man—
redeemed man, glorified man, sinless man—shall be
not only as the dust of the earth but as the stars of
heaven for multitude. In the coming day the number
of the lost will be forgotten, so infinitesimal in comparison with the company of the redeemed, increased
to a countless multitude yet gathered about one center
—"the praise of the glory of His grace." What a story
these peoples and their inherited heavenly spheres will
tell through eternity!

"An Holy Temple in the Lord"

We shall miss the purport and progress of this chapter unless we pause to remind ourselves that God's pur-

pose in thus constituting His household of Jew and Gentile, on a basis of coequality, is to cause them to be not merely His family but the building that houses His family. This purpose is disclosed in the threefold statement of theme at the conclusion of Chapter 2. It passes from the household to the building, the foundation of which is Christ, "in whom all the building fitly framed together groweth unto an holy temple in the Lord" (2:21).

So then we have become His New-Covenant Temple, that upon which His name is named and with which His glory is henceforth associated. But the distinctive feature of this temple is that Christ by His Cross removed its partitions (2:14)—no longer an inner court for Jews and an outer for Gentiles; and now He has become Himself its "Chief corner stone," that which unites each several part, so that we are one in Him.

This leads to the third and concluding step, that we as His temple "are builded together for an habitation of God through the Spirit" (2:22). God appointed the Tabernacle as the meeting-place for Himself and His people. To this end He came and dwelt in it. So He says to His New-Testament people: "What agreement hath the temple of God with idols? for ye are the temple of the living God; as God hath said, I will dwell in them, and walk in them" (2 Cor. 6:16).

That God would accept the fruit of His gospel; claim them as His temple; possess them as His abode in the Spirit; that they should actually experience His indwelling and inwalking presence—this is the burden and intent of Paul's prayer. He is presenting in dedicatory prayer the temple he has been helping to rear.

2—Paul's Prayer in Dedication of the Temple That God's Presence May Fill the House, 3:14-21

Note

A comparison of Paul's Prayers in Chapter 1 and here, will aid us in grasping the progress of the teaching:

IN CHAPTER 1	IN CHAPTER 3
He Prays for KNOWLEDGE	He prays for EXPERIENCE
There—"GOD IS LIGHT"	Here—"GOD IS LOVE"
He asks for LIGHT	He asks for LOVE
concerning	experienced by
HIS POWER and PROVISION	His Presence
for us	in us
It is the NEW MAN IN	It is the NEW MAN ON
HEAVEN	EARTH
In the PRESENCE OF GOD	God's PRESENCE IN HIM
It is the MAN IN GLORY	It is the GLORY IN MAN

PRAYER TO THE FATHER (3:14, 15). This is the one authorized form of address in the New Testament. We cannot too frequently remind ourselves of the order: To the Father; in the name of the Son; by, in, and through the Spirit. But there is peculiar significance in the address in the present prayer: His new family is being presented to Him for blessing. So the phrase is added: "Of whom all familyhood is named." The inner meaning cannot well be expressed in translation; it is hidden in the relation of the two words, *pater,* father, and *patria,* family. It states that the family comes from God (a fact that finds fullness of meaning in our Chap. V), and this relationship is embodied in the further fact that the family bears His name.

THE THREEFOLD FULLNESS (3:16-19). Once again the blessings of the gospel are conveyed to us in terms of the Trinity: 1—Inward strengthening by the Spirit (16); 2—The experience of the indwelling Christ

(17) ; 3—The fullness of God (19). As salvation came to us by the combined working of Father, Son, and Spirit (Eph. 1:3-14), so now its truths are to be transmuted into living experience, and that of the highest order, by the same Trinity in a unison of blessing.

Only, now, their working is not objective and outward, but subjective and inward. The identification of the saved and the Saviour, *taught* in all that has preceded, is now to become an experienced reality. That we should be "in Him" is but half of the story; the relationship is complete and of power only as He is "in us." This twofold identification is at the heart of Jesus' teaching, and He gave it in one breath: "Abide in Me, and I in you."

This Abiding Life is normally expressed as the Indwelling of the Spirit; it is He who was promised to make His abode with us and in us. But His coming is not singly; it is that Christ may indwell us, and likewise the Father. So Jesus our Lord taught and promised:

"And I will pray the Father, and He shall give you another Comforter, that He may abide with you for ever" (John 14:16).
"If a man love Me, he will keep My words: and My Father will love him, and We will come unto him, and make Our abode with him" (John 14:23).

Upon these words of promise Paul bases his petition, simply asking that what is their covenant right may become their Christian experience. (Cf. Romans 8, where the victorious life of the believer is portrayed as one of relationship to Christ, to the Spirit, to the Father.)

Strengthened by the Spirit (16). This is not a prayer for the incoming of the Spirit, for since the day of Pentecost no one believes upon Christ as his Saviour without receiving at once the gift of the Spirit as the covenanted response of the Father to his faith (see Gal.

4:6; 1 Cor. 12:13; Rom. 8:9). God knows it is an impossibility for any one to live a Christian life apart from the Holy Spirit.

But now Paul asks that they may experience the strengthening of the Spirit, and that "in the inner man." He would have the spiritual nature quickened and fortified against the flesh, that they may live in the Spirit, fulfilling the desires, not of the flesh but of the Spirit. This benefit is sought from the abounding resources of God, "according to His riches in glory," a phrase which Paul uses with the Philippians to assure them, and us, that out of that exhaustless supply He would supply all their need.

The Indwelling Christ and His Love (17-19). Again, it is not a prayer that Christ may come into the heart of the believer, as though He were a stranger to it; rather is it a prayer for the *experience* of His indwelling, with the spiritual values that flow from such an experience.

"By faith," not by feeling, for this is variable and must often breed misgivings. Faith rests on God's Word: "Faith cometh by hearing . . . the Word of God" (Rom. 10:17). The Word assures the believer that Christ is in the heart. Faith rests upon this revealed fact and, counting it true, appropriates Christ— the indwelling Christ—for its every need. Thus faith becomes the key to a wondrous, transforming experience of Christ and His love in the heart-life.

"Grounded and Founded in Love" (17b). Thus rendered these two words become architectural terms, referring to the temple which the Apostle is desiring to perfect as He presents it to the Father. Others render, "rooted and founded"; then the latter refers to the temple and the former to the vine that is a part of its adornment.   The latter rendering is perhaps to be preferred as it brings us into the Vine-and-Branch teaching, the heart of which is love, as the means of realizing that love in terms of temple dimensions.

THE BREADTH, LENGTH, DEPTH, HEIGHT (18). As in the figure of the Body of Christ its full stature height is to be realized by love as its growth principle (4:15, 16), so here under the figure of the Building; its temple, proportions, worthy of the glorious Presence, come to be realized by the expansive experience of love in each believer's heart.   Properly speaking the individual believer is the "living stone" in the temple.   Collectively they form the whole; but the whole will be only what each component stone enables it to become.

So the Apostle prays for this experience in common "with all the saints."   This being made "strong to comprehend" the love of Christ is the privilege, not of the few, but of all, by right and heritage.   Only as all enter into their privileged experience can the building be "fitly framed together," cemented in love and "grow into an holy temple in the Lord," by the love that excludes the things inimical to spiritual life.

> I love Thee, Lord; yet 'tis no love of mine
> That goeth forth to that great heart of Thine:
> 'Tis Thine own love which Thou hast given me
> Returning back, O loving Lord, to Thee.
>
> Naught but Thy love can satisfy my heart,
> Constrain my will from self and sin to part;
> In love so great Thou giv'st Thyself to me;
> For Thou art Love—to all eternity.
>
> Oh! help me, Lord, to take, by grace divine,
> Yet more and more of that great love of Thine;
> That day by day my heart may give to Thee
> A deeper love and growing constantly.
>
> *—Rev. J. Mountain.*

Knowing the Love that Passeth Knowledge (19a). It is not a prayer that we know the unknowable: Christ's love is not that. It is a prayer that we may know by experience what cannot be entered into as a mere matter of knowledge. Love planted in the heart has its reasons, more discerning than mere reasoning. Yet, however much we may taste and prove the love of Christ, still it "passeth knowledge" in the sense that its unexplored boundaries must ever lie far out beyond us.

"Filled unto All the Fulness of God" (3:19b). The word for *fullness* is one of the trenchant words of New-Testament Greek. Christ is "the fulness of the Godhead." The Church, as His Body, is "the fulness of Him that filleth all in all." And now that we have become to Him all that we are in His plan of the ages, it is proposed—and made possible—that by His indwelling presence we should be *filled unto all His fullness.* Seemingly He is prepared to give *Himself* to us, nothing withheld, in transforming presence. Only as we are filled with His fullness can we fulfill our calling, that of being "the fulness of Him that filleth all in all."

Comment

The Strengthening of the Spirit is the paramount need of every believer, not so much for the doing of great deeds as for the day-by-day realizing of the Christlike life. Not one of us can live a truly Christian life upon his own resources. The finer qualities, the mark of the genuine, these are the fruit of the Spirit's inward strengthening. Listen! "Strengthened with all might according to His glorious power, unto all patience and longsuffering with joyfulness" (Col. 1:11).

We need to place a higher value upon the things of

the Spirit. One day a little office boy, twitted by his employers for being so small, rebuked them by saying: "But I can do what you men can't do." Asked what that might be, he replied: "I can talk without swearing." In the tests of life can we suffer with patience? Forebear in silence? And that, "with joyfulness"?

THE LOVE OF CHRIST is the love of the God of love which He came to earth to express some nineteen hundred years ago. The dimensions of that love are embodied in these best-loved words—John 3:16:

ITS BREADTH—"For God so loved the world,"

ITS LENGTH—"That He gave His only begotten Son,"

ITS DEPTH—"That whosoever believeth in Him should not perish,"

ITS HEIGHT—"But have everlasting life."

Then the New Man on earth, who is now in heaven, walked among men with such love as this, even unto death. And now, having acquired a New Man to take His place down here, He is pouring His life, His very Self, into us, that we may live and love with His love— the very same.

It passeth knowledge, that dear love of Thine,
My Jesus, Saviour; yet this soul of mine
Would of Thy love, in all its breadth and length,
Its height and depth, its everlasting strength,
    Know more and more.
It passeth telling, that dear love of Thine,
My Jesus, Saviour; yet these lips of mine
Would fain proclaim to sinners far and near
A love which can remove all guilty fear,
    And love beget.
But though I cannot sing, or tell, or know
The fullness of Thy love, while here below,
My empty vessel I may freely bring:
O Thou, who art of love the living spring,
    My vessel fill.

> Oh, fill me, Jesus, Saviour, with Thy love!
> Lead, lead me to the living fount above;
> Thither may I, in simple faith, draw nigh,
> And never to another fountain fly,
>   But unto Thee.
>   —*Mary Shekleton.*

THE LIFE OF FULLNESS. God proposes to flood our lives with His fullness, that, filled with Himself, there shall not be found room for the fretful, shameful things of self. How often, viewing the tide-flats of some habited inlet, we have seen them strewn with unsightly evidences of human life. Then we have watched the tide come in, flooding and overflowing, till there was no room for aught but its beautiful, abounding fullness.

Such is the experience that our God waits to bring into the heart-life of all who are His own. It is a life that displaces self with Himself; that dispels the restless cravings of a dissatisfied life with the calm and quiet, the peace, the serenity of His sufficiency to satisfy. It is an experience of Himself, designed to keep the heart of His child centered in Him.

> O Christ, in Thee my soul hath found,
>   And found in Thee alone,
> The peace, the joy I sought so long,
>   The bliss till now unknown.
> Now, none but Christ can satisfy,
>   None other name for me;
> There's love, life, and lasting joy,
>   Lord Jesus, found in Thee.
>   —*B. E.*

The Doxology and Dedication, 3:20, 21
Note

THE LIMITLESS ONE (3:20a). This incomparable Epistle marks off the first portion of its message with another doxology. Thus it ends as it began. This doxology is an ascription of praise to our God as the hearer and answerer of prayer, limitless in resource. Phrase is piled upon phrase in the attempt adequately to depict His ability us-ward.

He is able to do *all* that we ask or even think.

He is able to do *above* all that we ask or think.

He is able to do *abundantly* above all that we ask or think.

He is able to do *exceeding* abundantly above all that we ask or think.

THE CHANNEL OF HIS POWER—OUR PERSONALITY

(3:20b). This is the amazing fact of the New Testament, that He has therein covenanted that His power, limitless as it is in itself, shall be so coupled with our personality, whom grace has so intimately identified with Him, that henceforth it shall flow through us as its channel. Great and glorious in majesty, He has voluntarily pressed His power into the mould of human personality, for under the terms of the New Covenant He cannot act independently of us, but in and through us, even as the head works through the body.

GLORY IN THE CHURCH (3:21). The prayer of dedication being ended, we reach the goal of it all—glory to our God. Paul, in presenting the temple of his building, desires the same token of acceptance as at Solomon's dedication. We read: "Now when Solomon had made an end of praying . . . the glory of the Lord filled the house. And the priests could not enter into the house of the Lord, because the glory of the Lord had filled the Lord's house" (2 Chron. 7:1, 2). Also, when the Tabernacle was finished and everything in place, "Then a cloud covered the tent of the congregation, and the glory of the Lord filled the tabernacle" (Ex. 40:34).

These are but types of the glory to be realized in His
New-Testament temple, which temple we are. Nor
yet a passing glory; rather, "glory in the Church by
Christ Jesus unto all the generations of the age of the
ages," for so it reads in the Greek. Eternity is made
up of ages, and the ages of generations. Through all
their duration and throughout all their expanse He has
His glory in the Church.   (

THE AMEN is seemingly the counterpart of an earlier
Amen at the conclusion of a similar doxology:
"Blessed be the Lord God of Israel from everlasting
to everlasting: and let all the people say, Amen" (Ps.
106:48).

Comment

OUR ABLE-ABUNDANTLY-ABOVE-ALL GOD. The
studies we have now concluded contain teachings that
stagger. How can they be true? How can they be
realized? The answer is the *ability* of 'God. Our
thought is turned to Him, with all the superlatives that
language can command. His ability, covering all past,
all present, all future, is superabounding.

Scripture asserts that "He is able—"; then fills in
the picture with our need. He is: able to deliver in
peril (Dan. 3:17); able to uphold in temptation (Heb.
2:18); able to heal the sick (Matt. 9:28); able to save
to the uttermost (Heb. 7:25); able to bring life from
death (Rom. 4:21); able to keep from falling (Jude
24); able to make all grace abound (2 Cor. 9:8). So
also is He able to carry out to the full this amazing
Ephesian program (Eph. 3:20). But, for the doing of
it He must have

OUR YIELDED LIVES. The case requires it. One cannot study Ephesians 1-3 without realizing that nothing
short of this will suffice. In solemn covenant He has

given Himself utterly to us; we must give ourselves in utterness to Him. Refusing, we render His plan inoperative—we hold the key. Yielding, pliant in His hand, answering spirit to Spirit, mind to Mind, will to Will, life to Life, love to Love—the result is heaven's glory in earthly mould.

Paganini, the world-famed violinist, was once playing before an audience when, in the midst of his brilliant performance, a string snapped. He played on, only to have a second fail him. With but two strings he continued his rendition. Then a third broke. With but one string at his command the master-player, unfaltering and undismayed, proceeded to the end with such brilliance and skill that his audience burst into a frenzy of applause. Paganini was but a man; our master-player is God. We may seem to ourselves to be of little use, dull and unresponsive, gifted with but a single string, yet if the instrument of our lives be wholly given up to Him, He will use it to bring forth heavenly glory under the power and skill of His touch.

> "Once it was my working,
> His it hence shall be;
> Once I tried to use Him,
> Now He uses me."

CHAPTER IV

THE MOST WONDERFUL WALK EVER UNDERTAKEN

EPHESIANS 4:1-5:20

The transition we have now reached is the clean-cut, decisive one of passing from Doctrine to Duty. Nor is it duty selected at random, by the whim of the writer or the suggestion of passing circumstance. It is duty that springs from the doctrine, answering to it and enforced by it. It is *the* duty that the doctrine calls for, as closely and vitally correspondent as are the branch and leaf of a tree to the root and trunk from which they derive their being and draw their life.

PAUL'S THEREFORES, standing as sentinels at the transition point of his Epistles, have the trenchant force of gathering into themselves all that has gone before of God's goodness embodied in doctrinal exposition and focusing it upon the heart and life in the irresistible appeal of practical exhortation. In the "therefore" the teaching of the doctrinal portion is held in solution, only to be precipitated into daily living in the practical portion that follows. E.g., Romans 12:1; Galatians 5:1.

How immeasurably we weaken the Word of God when we come to men with the duty, omitting the doctrine out of which it grows. The Church that turns away from doctrine is robbing its faith of divine reasonableness, resting it upon the shifting, superficial foundation of human appeal. The blunder is unpardonable, for the loss is irreparable. To harangue people into better living is one thing; to root our appeal in a relationship we sustain to Christ through the eternal purposes of grace is quite another. Pursuing the latter course, we could fill our Churches with intelligent believers, joyous in their faith, steadfast in good works.

The Christian's Walk is determined by these considerations. Not that he is to walk by some rule or standard of conduct—not that; but his walk is to conform to his relationship to Christ, to his standing in Him, to the fact that he is *His Very Own,* possessed of His nature, life, and presence. There is no arbitrary requirement, only the normal expression of a vital union. In Him we have our heavenly standing, rich and perfect in His riches and perfections. In us He must find His earthly walk, a true expression of Him who "dwells in us and walks in us" (2 Cor. 6:16).

In Him—We have our Standing in Heaven (Part I)

In Us—He has His Walking on Earth (Part II)

Outline

IV. Our Walking as the Body of Christ in Keeping with Our Standing, 4:1-5:20.

    1. We are to Walk Worthily, in Inward Realization of Christ, 4:1-16.

        a. Our calling to oneness of the Spirit (1-3).

        b. His provision for oneness {One Spirit (4). One Lord (5). One Father (6).

        c. His gifts to His Body (7-11).

            (1) Our responsibility according to Christ's gift (7).

            (2) Gifts bestowed through His triumphant ascension (8-10).

(Preceded by His "Descent" that He might lead all captivity captive (9, 10).)

(3) His gifts enumerated (11).

d. The intent of these gifts (12-16).

(1) The growth and unity of the Body (12, 13).
(Nothing short of a "perfect man, the measure of the stature of the fulness of Christ").

(2) This attainment is needful for us all (14-16).

(a) That we may escape the snares of dwarfed, protracted childhood (14).

(b) That we may grow up in all things into our Head (15).

(c) That from Him the whole Body may rightly function (16a) and build itself up in love (16b).

2. We are to Walk Differently, in Outward Manifestation of the Spirit, 4:17-32.

a. Not walk as the **Natural**, Unregenerate Man (17-19).

(1) What man is by nature (17b, 18).

(2) And therefore by practice (19).
Compare the same picture, expanded—Rom. 1:21-32.

b. Put off the **Carnal**, the "Old Man" (20-22).

(1) "Christ" means a different sort of life (20, 21).

(2) Calls for laying aside (as a garment) our former manner of life (22).

   c. Put on the **Spiritual,** the "New Man" (23, 24).

     (1) We must "be renewed in the spirit of our mind" (23).

     (2) Clothed with a new life, God-created, righteous and holy (24).

   d. Practical implications of this change of clothing (25-32). "Wherefore"

     (1) Put away lying; speak only truth (25).

     (2) Put away anger; defeat the devil (26, 27).

     (3) Put away stealing; work and give (28).

     (4) Put away worthless talk; speak good to edification (29).

     (5) Put away all that grieves the Spirit; be kind and forgiving as God has forgiven us (30-32).

3. We are to Walk Lovingly, in Upward Imitation of Our Father, 5:1-17.

As "Imitators of God"

   a. Walk as children of love* (1-7).

     (a) Having Christ as our Example (2).

     (b) Eschewing sensual practices (3, 4).

     (c) Those practicing such have no inheritance in His Kingdom (5).

     (d) But invite the wrath of God upon them (6, 7).

   b. Walk as children of light (8-14).

     (a) Thus to bring forth the fruit of the light (9).

---

*Not the phrasing of Scripture. The Greek says, "Children beloved."

   (b) Proving what is acceptable unto the Lord (10).
   (c) Refusing to fellowship with the unfruitful works of darkness (11a).
   (d) Rather reprove the shameful things done in secret (11b, 12).
   (e) For they require light to test and manifest them (13).
   (f) Exhortation to arise and come to Christ the Light (14).

  c. Walk as children of wisdom (15-17).
   (a) As wise and not unwise (15b).
   (b) Buying up the opportunity, since the times are evil (16).
   (c) Seeking the more to understand the Lord's will (17).

4. Secret and Summary of the Christian Walk, 5:18-20.

  a. A life filled with the Spirit (18).
  b. A heart overflowing with praise to the Lord (19).
  c. A spirit giving thanks always to the Father (20).

Chart: See opposite page.

WALKING expresses the duty and responsibility correspondent to our privileged Standing. The two must match. That his walking should measure up to his standing is the essence and goal of the believer's duty.

WORTHILY AS A BODY. We are "the Body of Christ," meant to represent Him truly, to express His mind and will, to live His life. This takes us back to Chapter 2, to the forming of the Body. But it also includes the truth we learned in Chapter 3. We are His Building,

Ephesians — HIS VERY OWN

STAND-ING			WALK-ING	WALK-ING	WAR-ING
CHAP. 1	CHAP. 2	CHAP. 3	4:1-5:20	5:21-6:9	6:10-24
AS HIS BELIEVERS	AS HIS BODY 1:22-23	AS HIS BUILDING 2:19-22	WORTHILY AS A BODY		
FATHER { CHOSE, ADOPTS, WILL ACCEPT } 1:3-6	QUICKENED BY THE GRACE OF GOD 2:1-10	HOUSEHOLD OF GOD 3:1-13 — MYSTERY OF THE AGES	ONE BODY (INWARD) STATURE OF CHRIST 4:1-16		
SON { PURCHASED, ENLIGHTENS, WILL INHERIT } 1:7-12	MADE ONE BY THE BLOOD OF CHRIST 2:11-17	TEMPLE IN THE LORD 3:6 — PARTITIONS REMOVED	NEW MAN (OUTWARD) FRUIT OF SPIRIT 4:17-32		
SPIRIT { SAVED, SEALS, WILL CLAIM } 1:13,14	ACCESS BY THE ONE SPIRIT 2:18	HABITATION IN THE SPIRIT 3:14-21 — FILLED WITH ALL GLORY	IN LOVE (UPWARD) IMITATORS OF GOD 5:1-20		
Prayer for Revelation / Power of Resurrection	HE—Our Peace / WE—Fellow citizens	Able Exceeding Abundantly Above all we ask AMEN	Gifts of CHRIST / Graces of SPIRIT / Glory of GOD	BRIDE—TO BE	AMEN

IN HIM — Our Standing in Heaven   IN US — His Walking on Earth

the temple for the indwelling of His presence. But
this building was designed for the Christian pilgrim-
age—it also walks. When the Israelites journeyed the
Tabernacle, carried by the Levites, actually walked in
their midst. So He says to us, and of us: "Ye are
the temple of the living God; as God hath said, I will
dwell in them and walk in them" (2 Cor. 6:16). We
are to express both the life (of the body), and the presence (of the building).

INWARDLY, in vital union with CHRIST, we must
realize His ONENESS of Spirit and FULLNESS of
growth. This, for the development of the BODY.

OUTWARDLY, our conduct must be expressive of the
new life within, the manifestation of the FRUIT OF THE
SPIRIT in daily living. This is the change of clothing,
suited to the NEW MAN.

UPWARDLY, our lives will be standardized by our
Father. As Imitators of God we will show forth the
family traits. Walking on earth in His likeness, as
His children we are bound to walk In Love.

THE THREEFOLD SUMMARY of the believer's Walk is
embodied in the last space:

(1) GIFTS OF CHRIST secure our oneness and growth
into Him.

(2) GRACES OF THE SPIRIT make manifest our walk
in newness of life.

(3) GLORY OF GOD ensures a life worthily expressive of His likeness.

The walk we have undertaken has a threefold obligation, in the living out of our relationship to Christ, to
the Spirit, to God the Father, as follows:

(1) WORTHILY. In Inward Oneness in Christ.

(2) DIFFERENTLY. In Outward Manifestation of
the Spirit.

(3) LOVINGLY. In Upward Patterning after God.

1—We Are to Walk Worthily, in Inward Realization of Christ, 4:1-16

Note

PAUL BESEECHES as "the prisoner in the Lord" (4:1), as though to enforce his appeal: "In the Lord's cause and by His appointive will I am bound. You who are free have the greater responsibility to use your freedom in walking worthily of Him."

WALKING WORTHY OF OUR CALLING (4:1-3). Scripture gives our calling a threefold description: 1—High (Phil. 3:14); 2—Holy (2 Tim. 1:9); 3—Heavenly (Heb. 3:1). Our walk, to be worthily in keeping with such a calling, must be: 1—"With all lowliness and meekness"; 2—"With longsuffering, forbearing one another in love"; 3—"Giving diligence to keep the unity of the Spirit in the bond of peace."

CHRISTIAN UNITY (4:3) is "of the Spirit." It is of His begetting. We are not asked to create it or legislate it. He provides it; we are to "keep" it.

OUR ONENESS IS IN THE TRINITY (4:4-6): One Spirit (4); one Lord (5); one Father (6). In Him, our triune God, there is no schism. The three are one and, working together, engender a true, genuine oneness among believers. From these three, as the basic primary elements, proceed four derived elements, constituting the sevenfold unity of Christian faith and practice—the only basis of union among believers.

THE GIFTS OF CHRIST (4:7) are the "measure" of spiritual responsibility. Bestowments of "grace," they nevertheless devolve upon "every one of us" a solemn responsibility for the trust reposed in us, for the accom-

plishment of its designed purpose. The varying measure, and the attendant accountability to Him, Jesus
taught in His parables of the Talents and the Pounds
(Matt. 25:14-30; Luke 19:12-27).

These gifts are the direct outcome of His glorious
victory (8-10). Having triumphed over His foes and
ours, from the lowest depths to the highest heights,
none escaping (9, 10), He "led captivity captive"—a
description of the powers of evil that once held us captive, now made captive by Christ's redemptive triumph.
This done, He "gave gifts unto men," that they might
share His victory, set free with a blessed freedom—
severed from Satan, and bound to Christ, eternally His
in life and destiny.

THE SPECIFIC GIFTS are now enumerated (4:11),
men whom He "gave," with the sense of "appointed"
or "ordained" to their allotted work. He "gifted" them
to the Church. "Some, apostles"—an office that in the
nature of its qualifications could not be perpetual (be-
ware of those who claim to have apostles today);
"some, prophets," communicating the revealed mind
and will of God to men; "some, evangelists," itinerant,
pioneers, missionaries, bearing the Good News to new
and distant fields; "some, pastors and teachers," united
here in one classification, the gift to the individual
Church as the foregoing are to the Church at large,
charged with duties both spiritual and doctrinal. (The
governmental duties—cf. "bishop" or "elder" (1 Tim.
3)—are implied but not specified since Ephesians never
views the Church as an organization.)

From these specified "gifts," responsibility passes "to
every one of us" (7), so to receive them and respond
to their ministry that the entire body shall be built up
into the Head.

THE PURPOSE OF THE GIFTS (4:12-16). As stated, it is nothing short of wonderful:

"For the perfecting of the saints, for the work of the ministry, for the edifying of the body of Christ: till we all come in the unity of the faith, and of the knowledge of the Son of God, unto a perfect man, unto the measure of the stature of the fulness of Christ" (12, 13).

The "body of Christ" must come to its full stature, even "the fulness of Christ." To this end there must be a diligent "perfecting of the saints," and this, "unto the work of ministering," that so the body of Christ may be built up (12).

This is in purposeful preparation, a present anticipation if not realization, of a destined day—"till"—in which we shall "come to the unity of the faith and of the knowledge of the Son of God." The key to this is the Sonship of Christ, into which we enter as a progressive experience.

"We may discover three forms or degrees to His Sonship. His eternal Sonship is the basis of election, His Sonship by the Holy Ghost (Luke 1:35) is the basis of regeneration, and His Sonship from the grave (Rev. 1:5; Col. 1:18, ect.) is the form and fountainhead of the first resurrection" (Graham).

Thus the culmination, the terminus of the "till," in the present process of realizing His "stature," will be our fuller sonship in the experience of His promised appearing, when we "shall see Him as He is" and be made "like Him" in a "fulness" to which we can only approach in this life.

THE NECESSITY FOR GROWTH INTO HIS STATURE (4:14-16) is both negative and positive. Negatively— to escape a state of protracted spiritual infancy, affected by the varying winds of doctrine, preyed upon by the designs of deceitful men (how startlingly modern the picture). Positively—in the words of Scripture:

"But speaking truth in love, may grow up in all things into Him, who is the Head, even Christ; from whom all the body fitly framed and knit together through that which every joint supplieth, according to the working in due measure of each several part, maketh the increase of the body unto the building up of itself in love" (15, 16, R. V.).

Above it was the "stature" of the body; now it is the "spirit" that actuates it. The growth is wholly and intensely inward, in the nature and life of Him who "is love." So the picture is framed "in love" (first and last). The body, in all things growing up into the Head, partakes of His life and likeness, and "the whole," through the faithful functioning of every member, every joint supplying its own part, "builds itself up in love." A most wonderful body, being developed and endowed for a most wonderful walk!

Comment

ORGANIC UNION is much spoken of in our day. It contemplates the union of organized Churches, now governmentally separate. It is man's proposal as a remedy for the confessed evils of multiplied church denominations. Yet "organic" has to do with an organism, something vital, not with an organization, which is something mechanical. Ephesian truth is God's remedy for divisions among believers. It contemplates the Church solely as an organism, vitally united to Christ the Head. And then united to the Head, as members of His body, all believers find their oneness with each other. In gatherings where Christ and His Word are freely exalted, such a union of believers is experienced, with a most blessed fellowship, both edifying and satisfying.

THE CHRISTIAN MINISTRY. The exhortation to walk worthily comes home with peculiar force to the ministry, in its thought of itself and in the Church's attitude toward it, in view of the double fact: first, it is the gift of Christ to His Church; second, it occupies a key position in the Church's development, mediating between the Head and the Body. No higher conception is presented by the Scriptures than this in Ephesians. Yet, today, low estimates of the ministerial office are gaining currency, variously caused by secularizing influences, within and without the Church, by the stultifying of the sacred office through the bearers making use of it to selfish ends, savoring of unworthy motives, or to promulgating teachings that fail to represent, or that positively misrepresent, the Son of God, the chosen, exalted and glorious Head.

The antidote is evident. It is here before us. Let the minister accept His office as from Christ, a direct, divine appointment. Let him regard himself as Christ's gift to the Church. Let him strive always to please Him who chose and called him, careful to be in the place of His selecting, and, withal, content therein. Likewise, let the Church receive the minister as from the Lord, standing in reverence at His word: "He that receiveth whomsoever I send receiveth Me" (John 13: 20). Let them wait diligently on his ministry. Let them pray for him, upholding him with love in the Lord. Let them refuse to him anything that would tend to subvert or secularize his high calling. Let them show a worthy walk as the chief reward of his labors. God speed the day!

"SPEAKING THE TRUTH IN LOVE." Somehow many seemingly content themselves with striving to speak the truth. They feel themselves at liberty to speak out, if they but hold to the truth. Such utterance is not the Scripture. The truth, if spoken, is to be "in love." Truth is not enough; we must have, and hold to, the "Spirit of truth" (1 John 4:6). Regard for this limitation would leave much unsaid. And if spoken in faithfulness to this standard, robbed of its sting, it would bring an unwonted blessing.

The position of these words in Scripture, in connection with the development of Christ's body, is deeply significant. Undoubtedly the disregard of them, even in zeal for the truth as we see it, is responsible for both a dividing of the Body, robbing it of its oneness in Christ, and a dwarfing of the Body, depriving it of the love that is its essential, up-building quality. We who love the truth should be particularly careful to commend it by speaking it "in love."

The Body Building Itself up in Love. The Church is possessed of a native life-force, imparted by the Spirit from Christ its Head, which acts as a perennial source of growth. It functions as the life-blood, however, only as it can flow unhindered through every part of the body. Each member and each joint must do its part in supplying the vital fluid. So it is in the natural body; so in the Body of Christ.

We are in a relation of interdependence. Some are more responsibly situated than others. The wrist, for example, is responsible for the life-flow to the hand and fingers beyond it. If it fails they must atrophy. The elbow cannot live to itself nor die to itself. It has in its keeping the blood and nerve force that are the very life of forearm, hand, fingers, all lying beyond it. And the shoulder holds the key to all these; through it they must receive whatever measure of life and strength is theirs.

Dear reader, what is your place of responsibility in the Body? Are you to others as a shoulder? an elbow? Do they live or die through you? Is the Body of Christ dwarfed by your anemia, your lack of vital, spiritual corpuscles? Or is it maimed through your neglect, separating yourself, in whatsoever degree, from fellowship with the Head? Or, may it be, that through what you are supplying of spiritual life and love, the Body is growing up into the Head, getting to itself new strength, suffused into all its members, thereby "building itself up in love"? Happy he whose life is thus counting for the completion of the Body of Christ.

2—We Are to Walk Differently, in Outward Manifestation of the Spirit, 4:17-32

Note

Believers, built into the Body of Christ, are a "New Man" upon earth. Being such, they should exchange the clothing of the "Old Man" for new garb, thus to appear before the world in a true light. This, the outward manifestation of our inward union with Christ, yes, and with one another, is now before us.

Paul brings into review the three men, known to God, the natural man, the carnal man, the spiritual man (listed in 1 Cor. 2:14, 15; 3:1), with the "walk" that is normal to the life of each. We being in the Spirit, our walk must necessarily be different from that of the Natural and of the Carnal.

WE ARE NOT TO WALK AS THE NATURAL MAN (4: 17-19). Who are the Gentiles? The unregenerate, untouched by the Spirit of God. Consider his picture: 1—What man is by nature (17b, 18). His mind— "vanity"; his understanding—"darkened"; his heart— "blindness." 2—What he is, therefore, by practice (19). "Past feeling"; "given over to lasciviousness"; "working all uncleanness"; "with greediness."

The full portrait, with life-size features, is found in Romans 1:21-32. Sad to say, it is true, terribly true to life.

WE ARE TO PUT OFF THE CARNAL MAN (4:20-22).
We have "not so learned Christ" (20).   Christ—His
name stands for a new order of things, a new sort of
living.   Having "the truth in Jesus" (21), His teachings and example, we are bound to live true to Him, in
a totally different walk.   This calls for the "putting
off," the laying aside of the garments we were accus-
tomed to wearing, garments by which we were known,
suited to the former ways of the "old man," naturally
"corrupt" with "deceitful lusts" (22). Jesus, our Kins-
man-Redeemer, in wondrous humbling of Himself,
came to be like us that we, by wonderful grace, might
be found in His likeness.   Henceforth it is our privilege
to walk as becometh Him.

WE ARE TO PUT ON THE SPIRITUAL MAN (4:23,
24).   This man belongs to a new order.   He is "a new
creation," the "new man" of Ephesians.   This new man
is now to come to manifestation in Christian life and
character.   Therefore the first step is to "be renewed"
(23a), renewed from the ruin of the first creation; renewed not alone "in mind" (cf. vs. 17), but "in the
spirit of your mind" (23b).   The mind must be quickened by a new spirit actuating it.   Only so will our
life show itself different.   Only so will we "walk in
newness of life."   This is God's way of working, not
on the surface but from within out.

Then follows, on our part, the putting on of "the
new man" (24a), the outward manifestation of that
which God has inwardly wrought.   This man is: 1—
"after God," according to His electing will and purpose in redemption; 2—"created," a New-Covenant
miracle of God's creative work; 3—"in righteousness
and true holiness," in a new mould, to the exclusion
of sin's marrings and warpings in the old creation

(24b). This is the man we are to "put on," by a life in keeping, suited to making him manifest.

"WHEREFORE." This one word gathers into itself the practical implications of this change of clothing (4:25-32). Manifestly we must be different, but how? In what respects? What are the things regarding which we must exercise particular care? The Spirit specifies the following:

We must, 1—Put away lying. Our speech is one way in which we show the mind, the Spirit, the life within. Our inner life is begotten in truth; we must speak only truth (25). 2—Put away anger (26a). True, one may indulge a "righteous indignation" without sin (26b); but anger is of the working of the flesh (Gal. 5:19-21). To indulge it is to give the devil the place of control Christ alone should occupy (27). 3—Put away stealing (28a). Rather, by honest toil, we should manifest an earnest purpose in life (28b) and have wherewith to meet the need of others (28c). 4—Put away worthless talk (29a). Such "proceeding from the mouth," would misrepresent the new creation within (29b). Rather, our conversation should be chosen with a view to "edifying," building up believers, "ministering grace to the hearers" (29c). 5—Put away all that grieves the Spirit (30a), remembering that He has "sealed us unto the day of redemption" (30b). Meanwhile it is the Spirit who is working in us this new life. Hence the appeal for a life outwardly in keeping with the Spirit's in-working concludes with this summary:

"Let all bitterness, and wrath, and anger, and clamour, and evil speaking, be put away from you, with all malice: and be ye kind one to another, tenderhearted, forgiving one another, even as God for Christ's sake hath forgiven you" (31, 32).

For "Be kind" the literal rendering is "Become kind."

We cannot *be* kind until we *become* so by putting away
the things that are unkind. Further, "Forgiving one
another" is literally, "Forgiving yourselves"—one of
the finest possible reminders that Christian conduct
must constantly be tempered by the fact of the oneness
of believers in the body of Christ. So Alford para-
phrases thus: "Doing as a body for yourselves that
which God did once for you all."

Comment

THE CHRISTIAN'S DUTY TO BE DIFFERENT. Everything thus far in Ephesians converges upon the fact
that the believer *is* different, essentially and radically
different. Now he is called upon to make that difference manifest by his manner of life. The "therefore"
pivots upon this logical appeal: Since we are no longer
like others about us we are no longer to act like them.
We are asked merely to "be ourselves," acting out what
we are. One of these days we expect the difference to
be eternity wide. We would be unspeakably disap-
pointed if it were not. Then how reasonable is the
Gospel's requirement that we write that difference into
our present-day walk.

THE CHRISTIAN'S CHANGE OF CLOTHING. When
God creates a New Man and, instead of taking him immediately to his Glory Home, for purposes of testimony thrusts him forth into the world of men, He is
careful to play the part of a tailor in providing suitable
clothing for His son and heir to wear. His dress must
conform to his nature, position and purpose in life. So
the Father invites him into His robing room, not to
make but to *take* the articles of apparel most suited to
his person and station in life. And—let us not side-
step the argument from life—if the human body calls

for so large an expenditure of time, thought, effort and money that it may be appropriately and attractively attired, how much more the Body of Christ, that it may present a worthy appearance—worthy of Him—as it walks out before the world.

> "I want the adorning divine
>   Thou only, my God, canst bestow;
> I want in these beautiful garments to shine,
>   Which distinguish Thy household below."

THE CHRISTIAN'S CONFORMITY TO CHRIST. The highest sanction for a set-apart life, the chief consideration leading the believer so to live, is the fact of his identification with Christ. Close, intimate, inseparable, as the body is identified with the head—men never think of one apart from the other—such is our relationship to Christ. When men see us they see Him. What they think of us they inevitably think of Him. Dare we be anything less than Christ-like?

Then the process of putting off and putting on must continue until we are rid of all that is un-Christ-like and have reached the quintessence of Christliness—likeness to Him "who went about doing good"—in that we too are kind as He was kind, with a sympathetic kindness that is moved by the remembrance of His undeserved forgiveness.

Let Us Be Kind

> Let us be kind;
> The way is long and lonely,
> And human hearts are asking for this blessing only—
>   That we be kind.
> We cannot know the grief that men may borrow,
> We cannot see the souls storm-swept by sorrow,

But love can shine upon the way today, tomorrow—
    Let us be kind.

    Let us be kind;
This is a wealth that has no measure,
This is of Heaven and earth the highest treasure—
    Let us be kind.
A tender word, a smile of love in meeting.
 A song of hope and victory to those retreating,
A glimpse of God and brotherhood while life is fleeting—
    Let us be kind.

    Let us be kind;
Around the world the tears of time are falling,
And for the loved and lost these human hearts are calling—
    Let us be kind.
To age and youth let gracious words be spoken;
Upon the wheel of pain so many weary lives are broken,
We live in vain who give no tender token—
    Let us be kind.

    Let us be kind;
The sunset tints will soon be in the west,
Too late the flowers are laid then on the quiet breast—
    Let us be kind.
And when the angel guides have sought and found us,
Their hands shall link the broken ties of earth that bound us,
And Heaven and home shall brighten all around us—
    Let us be kind.

                —W. Lomax Childress

3—We Are to Walk Lovingly, in Upward Imitation of Our Father, 5:1-17

Note

The Body has been built up in inward appropriation of Christ, thus to attain His stature. It has been brought into the robing room for a suitable change of clothing, thus to walk out before the world in manifestation of the fruit of the Spirit. It must now relate its walk, its manner of life, to the Father, in an upward recognition of His character and earnestness of desire to be like Him.

Here there is an enriching of the imagery. While our duty Godward is set before us in a threefold reminder of the "walk" appropriate to the Body of His Son, the walk is to be consistent with the fact that we are His "children," the members of His family, His household upon earth, which is the figure of chapter 3. (Note that it thus forms a natural transition to our next study of the Family.)

A threefold family likeness, to reflect our Father rightly, must characterize His children: 1—Children of love, since "God is love"; 2—Children of light, since "God is light"; 3—Children of wisdom, since He is all-wise.

WALK AS CHILDREN OF LOVE (5:1-7). Why? And how? Doubtless the writer has in mind the very words of our Lord: "Love . . . that ye may be the children of your Father which is in heaven: for He maketh His sun to rise on the evil and on the good, and sendeth rain on the just and on the unjust" (Matt. 5:44, 45). God's love constantly displayed in the moral government of men, to the exclusion of resentment and wrath, must challenge His children to a like attitude at all times and under all circumstances. Yet the place where our Father's love is supremely displayed is in the person of His own Son. His love, historically expressed in the Cross and personally experienced in the believer, is the motivating power of the Christian walk.

This reason for walking in love is likewise the measure and manner of our love-walk: "Even as Christ

also loved you, and gave Himself up for us, an offering
and a sacrifice to God for an odor of a sweet smell"
(5:2, R. V.). The love of Christ is thus of a twofold
character: 1—Self-denying; His life, His all, He gave
up for us; 2—God-gratifying; His sacrifice was also
sweet-savored to God.

"But Fornication," etc. (5:3, 4) presents sin, the
sensual sins of the body, as entrenched in a life of
self-seeking and self-gratification. It is the opposite of
a life of love, brushing aside the principles by which
God manifested His love in making us His children.
Sin is a self-walk. Our deliverance from it will come
through walking in love, "even as Christ also loved":
1—Denying self, taking up our cross daily and following Him (Lu. 9:23); 2—Purposing so to live as to be
well-pleasing to our Heavenly Father. Otherwise we
discard all evidence that we are the children of His
love. For, listen!

No Inheritance—Wrath Is Coming (5:5-7).
The man who looks upon the Gospel of Grace, as embodied in our standing in Christ, as an easy way of slip-
ping into Heaven, irrespective of, yes in spite of, the
sort of life we live, here meets with disillusionment. He
finds himself "deceived with vain words" (vs. 6). Over
against them we may set the words of Paul, that the
provisions of the Gospel are directed to the end "that
the righteous requirement of the law might be fulfilled
in us, who walk not after the flesh, but after the Spirit"
(Rom. 8:4). Trusting in a faith unfruitful in life, one
meets the rebuff of James: "But wilt thou know, O
vain man, that faith without works is dead?" (Jas.
2:20). The wisdom of God is that we join hands with
Him in the two-sided seal of security: "Howbeit the
firm foundation of God standeth, having this seal, The

Lord knoweth them that are His: and, Let every one
that nameth the name of the Lord depart from un-
righteousness" (2 Tim. 2:19, R. V.). Failure to do this
merely fits one's life back into the picture of what we
were before grace found us—not children of love but
"children of disobedience" and "children of wrath" (cf.
vs. 6 with 2:2, 3).

WALK AS CHILDREN OF LIGHT (5:8-14). Appeal is
made to the radical change wrought by grace from
what we were, "once darkness," to what we are, "now
light in the Lord" (vs. 8). We are simply asked to be
natural, to be true to our new selves, to walk in keeping with what we are. Nor does such a walk result
from self-effort. Born of the Spirit, indwelt by the
Spirit, the fruit of the Spirit will find expression in our
lives, such as "goodness, righteousness and truth" (vs.
9). Thus we will be exhibiting upon earth our Father's
traits of character, thereby "proving what is acceptable
unto the Lord" (vs. 10).

SHUNNING THE WORKS OF DARKNESS (5:11, 12).
As in Galatians 5:19-23 the works of the flesh are opposed to the fruit of the Spirit, so here we meet the
same opposition; only they are appropriately described
as works of darkness. Deeds such as "it is a shame
even to speak of"—such doings instinctively seek the
sheltering cover of secrecy—done in the darkness to
which they are akin. With such works the children of
light can "have no fellowship." This is the very nature
of the case. Between light and darkness there is no
kinship. They are eternally at variance. Their sepa-
rateness by nature is so absolute and uncompromising
that John declares: "God is light and in Him is no
darkness at all. If we say that we have fellowship with
Him, and walk in darkness, we lie, and do not the
truth" (1 John 1:5, 6).

Light's Gospel Call (5:13, 14). There's another side to the story. Light must preserve itself, separate and unimpaired, not merely for its own sake but for the service it is in the world to render. It must search out the darkness, reprove it, draw it out into the open, with the aim and purpose of transforming it into light. Therefore the call that we, the children of light, are commissioned to issue in the name of our God to the children of darkness: 1—Awake, you who are sleeping through this night of the world's sin; 2—Arise from the dead, you who are in the grip of spiritual death; 3—Christ will give you the light of life.

Walk as Children of Wisdom (5:15-17). Here is the last occurrence of the word "Walk." It is a most significant one. We are addressed as those who should have their Father's heavenly wisdom: "not as unwise, but as wise." We are called upon to exhibit this wisdom by the fact that we "walk circumspectly." The Greek word means *accurately, pointedly,* that is, with the wisdom of a walk determined by a fixed, intelligent purpose. The wisdom that dictates such a walk is twofold: 1—the realization of what we are and are going to be, a wisdom imparted by the entire body of Ephesian truth; 2—the recognition of the evil all about us, wholly differing from us in both character and destiny.

This wisdom will lead us to be found "redeeming the time" (5:16a). The Greek says, "Buying up the opportunity," as though the opportunities for doing good were precious and all too fleeting. We might say, in the language of commerce, "Watching for a good buy."

The reason—"the days are evil" (5:16b). Surely they were at that time and are still, whether we estimate them by the intimate character of their deeds and purposes or from the standpoint of their attitude toward God, His gospel and His people. Any enumeration of the evil that the days have wrought would be appalling; yet it would fall far short of their sum, which is mounting daily. In the midst of it all God's children, as the children of wisdom, address themselves to "understanding what the will of the Lord is" (5: 17), that they may know it and walk in it.

Comment

THE NEED OF THE HOUR—GODLINESS. In a day when men are losing faith in God, which means He is Himself lost and unknown in His own world, the supreme service devolving upon His children is so to live that men meet Him again, as was the case with that other Son nineteen hundred years ago, in the life of a man. In a day of speculation we are called to remove our God from the realm of speculation to that of everyday, practical reality. In a day that preaches the doctrine of *doing*, writing its creed in terms of good deeds, God's people are called to hold the higher level of *being*, as the finest possible service to our generation. It is the renewed call to godliness—letting God become the warp and woof of life's thinking and living.

What a joy it is to step into a home where exists a family consciousness; where a family standard of ideals and aims of character and conduct is shared by all; where the heart and life of father and mother are reflected in the nobility of the children. It's a bit of heaven on earth. It is that touch of heaven that we are asked to bring into earthly circles by a life that is the conscious and consistent reflecting of the Father by His children.

Godliness—what are its constituent elements? Where

can they be found in truer portraiture than in this portion of Ephesians?

(1) UNSELFISHNESS. The citadel of sin is self. Why should any one wish to sin but that self might be gratified? The undoing of sin, to the enthroning of God, is the denying of self. Nowhere did the Son of God display His Godliness so fully as in giving up what He was to become man. As a man every step to the Cross, in the setting aside of self, was a manifesting of godliness. His whole life before men was a whispering to God: "None of self and all of Thee." At its close He could give its sum in saying to the Father: "I have glorified *Thee* on the earth."

(2) HOLINESS. God is a separated being. Those in His presence worship before Him, crying, "Holy, holy, holy." His favorite name for Himself is *The Holy One of Israel.* His favorite name for us is *His Holy Ones,* saints, set apart, separated. His favorite figure for enforcing this is the family tie, the binding of two lives in the marriage bond—set apart *to* each other *from* all others. How gladly, then, should the children of God accept their separatedness and live it out as the natural expression of their hidden relationship to Him—glad to be counted godly in testimony to an ungodly world.

(3) POINTEDNESS OF PURPOSE. In a world of men characterized by carelessness, aimlessness and laxity of living, the Christian should be outstanding for his fixity of purpose, for the worthwhileness of the things engaging his time and effort. His vision must be far-ranged. To strike a straight course across a field one should not drop his eyes—so doing his steps will zigzag—but fasten them upon his distant objective. So the child of God must walk as a partner in the plans of God, with the goal of oncoming ages filling his eye,

evaluating all about him in the fading light of time and the dawning of eternity. Living as having no time to lose, his soul-earnestness must be evident to all.

Redeem the Time

The time is short!
If thou wouldst work for God, it must be now;
If thou wouldst win the garland for thy brow;
Redeem the time!
Shake off earth's sloth!
Go forth with staff in hand while yet 'tis day;
Set out with girdled loins upon the way;
Up! Linger not!
Withstand the foe;
Die daily, that forever thou mayest live;
Be faithful unto death! the Lord will give
The crown of life.—*Horatius Bonar.*

Secret and Summary of the Christian Walk, 5:18-20
In reading these three significant verses we note that they sum up the walk in terms of the Trinity. Thus we meet again this characteristic of Ephesian truth and experience. Before examining them the reader is asked to go over the ground our walk has taken us as similarly summarized at the bottom of the chart (page 107).

1—THE GIFTS OF CHRIST—4:1-16.
By these the Body is built up, its inward need met.

2—THE GRACES OF THE SPIRIT—4:17-32.
Manifesting His presence outwardly by a changed life.

3—THE GLORY OF THE FATHER—5:1-17.
Reflecting His likeness in a godly manner of life.

So now, as we come to these closing words, we are bidden to find the secret of such a walk in

(1) A Life Filled with the Spirit (5:18). The Spirit is the supreme gift of Christ to His Church; through Him all other gifts minister. Without Him the Body would be lifeless and incapable of being up-built. Filled with the Spirit the flesh-life recedes, the Christ-life comes to fullness of power. It is a command to which all believers must give heed: until it is true of us our lives will lack the quality of being pleasing to Him. We *must* "Be filled with the Spirit."

(2) A Heart Overflowing with Praise to the Lord (5:19). A singing heart! What a secret! No surer way to guarantee a transformation of life. When the fullness of the Spirit fills the heart with our Saviour's praises, the lips will catch the overflow and the life will be swung into line. We will walk as we sing and talk. Nor will the fountain of life, thus fed, ever run dry.

(3) A Spirit Giving Thanks Always to the Father (5:20). This we could not do except for the fullness of the Spirit and our position in Christ, untouched by shifting circumstance. So we are bidden: "In everything give thanks: for this is the will of God in Christ Jesus concerning you" (1 Thess: 5:18). What a will this is! But if our Father has willed it, He has also made it possible "in Christ Jesus." It is that He may be glorified by the son of His love, as by that other Son. "By Him therefore let us offer the sacrifice of praise to God continually, that is, the fruit of our lips giving thanks to His name" (Heb. 13:15). Always —in everything—continually; our Father asks for a continuous flow of thanksgiving from His children. Is He not worthy? Shall He not have it, even from us? **Let us so walk.**

CHAPTER V

THE MOST WONDERFUL BRIDE EVER WOOED AND WON

EPHESIANS 5:21-6:9

With this section of Ephesians we pass from the more general relationships of life to the more special and intimate ties of the home. In the application of the exalted teachings of the doctrinal portion we are to find a new sacredness attaching to the family and a new motive for maintaining family relationships on a high plane of purity and nobility.

We should remind ourselves that there are just two divinely appointed social units: the Family, which is society in nature, and the Church, which is society in grace. In this chapter God uses the latter, with its sacred relationships, to purify and ennoble the former; again, He uses the familiar ties of the former to illustrate His glorious purposes in the latter.

In Christ we have become "the household of God" (Eph. 2:19). The original of that household, the prototype of the family circle, consisted of the Father, the Son, and the Holy Spirit. Creation contemplated the enlargement of the circle to include man. Adam created in the likeness of God, is called "the son of God." Sin robbed man of his heritage, in the home and heart of God. It robbed God, as well, of His children by creation. But, as we are soon to see, mirrored in the manner of forming the woman and presenting her

to the man—Adam and Eve the first family—was the
eternal purpose of God in Christ, in the Church, in
redemption. He would yet get to Himself a race, men
and women, "in His image, after His likeness," who
would be *His Very Own,* His household in whom is
all His delight.

This means that our earthly family relationships are
sanctified anew to the high and holy purpose of reflecting upon earth the beauties and glories of the heavenly
family of which we have become a part.

No Christian, then, can look upon his home as a
mere human convenience, a place where certain persons are privileged to live together in the enjoyment
of endearing family ties. Henceforth these home bonds
must be to us the sacred, God-appointed medium for
making manifest the heavenly harmonies. We are to
live and walk in the earthly family circle as members
of the heavenly family. We are so to order our home
life that it shall be both a type and a testimony; that
through it men shall see Christ in relationship to His
Church, see the Father in relationship to His children,
see the Holy Spirit in relationship to those who live
and serve through Him.

While all three relationships are fully dealt with,
that of Christ to His Church takes the evident pre-
eminence. Hence the title of this chapter.

Outline

**V. Our Walking in Earthly Relationships in Keep-
ing with Our Heavenly Standing, 5:21-6:9.**
We are to submit ourselves one to another (21).

  **1. As Wives and Husbands We Are the Bride of
  Christ, 5:22-33.**
  a. Wives are to submit to their husbands (22-
  24).

        (1) The manner: as unto the Lord (22b).
        (2) The reason: the headship of the husband (23a).
            Correspondent to the Headship of Christ (23b).
        (3) The duty solemnly enjoined (24).

   b. Husbands are to love their wives (25-30).
        (1) The manner: as Christ loved the Church (25-27).
            (a) Giving Himself for it (past) (25b).
            (b) Sanctifying and cleansing it (present) (26).
            (c) Presenting it to Himself glorious and flawless (future) (27).
        (2) The reason: the wife is his body (28a).
            (a) He is but loving himself (28b, 29a).
            (b) The same as "the Christ" and "the Church" (29b, 30).

   c. The sacred implications of Christian marriage (31-33).
        (1) An intimate, indissoluble union (31).
        (2) The mystery of Christian marriage— A picturing of Christ and the Church —His Bride (32).
        (3) The mutual obligation of love and reverence (33).

2. As Children and Parents We Are Children of Our Heavenly Father, 6:1-4.
   a. Children are to obey their parents (1-3).
        (1) The manner: "in the Lord (1a).
        (2) The reason: "for this is right" (1b).
        (3) Duty enjoined by "the first commandment with promise" (2, 3).

---

   2. Fathers' Christian duty to their children (4).

      (1) To "not provoke them to wrath" (4a).

      (2) To "bring them up in the nurture and admonition of the Lord" (4b).

3. As Servants and Masters We Serve Our Lord and Master, 6:5-9.

   a. Servants are to be obedient to their masters (5-8).

      (1) The manner: as unto Christ and not unto men (5b-7).

      (2) The reason: we shall receive it back again from the Lord (8).

   b. Masters are to be governed likewise in their relation to servants (9).

      (1) The manner: do the same, forbearing threatening (9a).

      (2) The reason: their Master is in Heaven (9b)—He is no Respecter of persons (9c).

Chart—See opposite page.

Heavenly As a Family sets forth the supreme obligation of the family, so to walk therein, collectively and individually, that our heavenly standing in Christ shall be reflected in these earthly ties.

The Trinity. In the four preceding sections the Trinity is the outstanding feature. Not so here. Are we to infer that it is absent? Far from it. In this section the Trinity is presented in picture. It would be superfluous, as well as poor taste, to add their names. (We recall the boy who, having drawn a horse, labeled it, "This is a horse." No such need in God's word-pictures.) Following down the chart, we can recognize: 1—Christ, in relationship to His Church; 2—The Father, in relationship to His children; 3—The

~ Ephesians ~
HIS VERY OWN

	STAND-ING			WALK-ING		WAR-ING
	CHAP. 1	CHAP. 2	CHAP. 3	4:1-5:20	5:21-6:9	6:10-24
	AS HIS **BELIEVERS**	AS HIS **BODY** 1:22-23	AS HIS **BUILDING** 2:19-22	**WORTHILY** AS A **BODY**	**HEAVENLY** AS A FAMILY	
FATHER { CHOSE / ADOPTS WILL / ACCEPT 1:3-6		QUICKENED BY THE **GRACE** OF **GOD** 2:1-10	HOUSEHOLD OF **GOD** 3:1-13 — MYSTERY OF THE AGES	ONE BODY (INWARD) STATURE of **CHRIST** 4:1-16	WIVES AND HUSBANDS 5:22-33	
SON { PURCHASED / ENLIGHTENS WILL / INHERIT 1:7-12		MADE ONE BY THE **BLOOD** OF **CHRIST** 2:11-17	TEMPLE IN THE **LORD** 3:6 — PARTITIONS REMOVED	NEW MAN (OUTWARD) FRUIT of **SPIRIT** 4:17-32	CHILDREN AND PARENTS 6:1-4	
SPIRIT { SAVED / SEALS WILL / CLAIM 1:13,14		ACCESS BY THE **ONE SPIRIT** 2:18	HABITATION IN THE **SPIRIT** 3:14-21 — FILLED WITH GLORY	IN LOVE (UPWARD) IMITATORS of **GOD** 5:1-20	SERVANTS AND MASTERS 6:5-9	
	Drayer for **R**evelation / **P**ower of **R**esurrection	HE—Our Peace / WE—Fellowcitizens	**A**ble Exceeding **A**bundantly **A**bove all we ask AMEN	**G**ifts of **CHRIST** **G**races of **SPIRIT** **G**lory of **GOD**	**B**RIDE— TO BE 5:31,32	AMEN
	IN HIM — *Our Standing in Heaven*			IN US — *His Walking on Earth*		

133

Holy Spirit, in relationship to those who serve in and through Him.

Wives, Children, Servants. In each instance these are placed first, reversing the order in which we naturally speak of these relationships. For example, we say "Husband and wife." Why this reversal? Because wives, children, servants, in each instance represent and typify the human responsibility in the respective relationships. They exemplify, in relationship, the Christian's walk, in his positional relation to Christ, Father, Spirit.

Note—the wife is "the body," carrying forward the entire teaching of the Body of Christ and its walking worthily of Him.

Bride-To-Be constitutes the appeal of this section. Living now in the light and prospect of that glorious consummation of our present relationship to Him—thus only shall we walk worthily of Him who chose and wooed us as *His Very Own.*

Introducing this division is the simple statement of the general principle of conduct which is to regulate our acts and attitudes toward each other, if they would be Christlike and God-glorifying: "Submitting yourselves one to another in the fear of God" (5:21).

1—As Wives and Husbands, We Are the Bride of Christ, 5:22-33

Note

Wives are to Submit Themselves unto their Husbands (5:22-24). It does not say, "obey." This is reserved for children and servants. The wife-to-husband relation is of a different order—more intimate, inward, vital, as embodied in the words, "your own." It is submission to our own—our very own, which is the appeal of Ephesians—not to another. Submitting to our own does not degrade us. The body is never degraded by submitting to its own head. It honors itself in so doing, for its positional relationship to the head calls for submission. So with the wife toward her own huband.

THE MANNER: "As unto the Lord" (22b). We are not suffered to lose sight for an instant of the higher reach and reference of life. We are not merely submitting to a man upon earth. We stand with reference to the husband as the Christian to Christ. This relationship is daily sanctified by its daily opportunity so to walk as to testify to Him—"as unto the Lord."

THE REASON lies in the headship of the husband (23a), correspondent to the headship of Christ over the Church (23b). God gave Christ to be Head of the Church. So likewise He gave man to be the head of the wife. No personal inferiority is implied. Position only is in question. There cannot be two heads; neither can the body assume the position of the head. Its position calls for submission. But the reason stated is not physical or intellectual; it is higher, in the realm of the spiritual.

THE DUTY IS SOLEMNLY ENJOINED (24), in words so conclusive as to rule out all question or argument:

"Therefore as the Church is subject unto Christ, so let the wives be to their own husbands in every thing."

Does the wife feel that she is being severely dealt with? Is more required of her in relation to her husband than might reasonably be expected? Let her listen while her husband is given his directions for earthly living by this heavenly standard. Let her listen and realize that the matter is wholly mutual, and that the husband has the heavier exactions since he stands in the place of Christ. Than this there is nothing higher on earth.

HUSBANDS ARE TO LOVE THEIR WIVES (5:25-30). Love! No word so fully embodies the Gospel. No act so adequately represents the Christ of our salvation.

THE MANNER: "As Christ loved the Church" (25-27). What a standard! The wife may well submit herself to a husband who loves as Christ loved. His love knows no bounds and no barriers. We are reminded what He has done, is doing, will do, in His love for the Church:

> Past—in His love, "He gave Himself up for it" (25).
>
> Present—in His love, He is "sanctifying and cleansing it with the washing of water by the Word" (26).
>
> Future—in His love, He purposes Himself to "present it to Himself a glorious Church, not having spot, or wrinkle, or any such thing" (27).

His love saved it, is sanctifying it, will glorify it. His love, unmindful of its faults, transforms it into a thing of beauty, that at last He himself—His love refuses to any other the privilege—may present the Church to Himself in holy faultlessness, one with Him in life and destiny—His Bride, *His Very Own.*

THE REASON men should love their wives: "So ought men to love their wives as their own bodies" (28a). The wife is his body. This is the exact counterpart of the wife's reason for submitting to her husband. They are complementary: the head to the body, the body to the head. More: to "your own" husbands corresponds "their own" bodies. He is merely loving his own.

This reason, however, is finally pressed to a yet more intimate issue—not loving "his own" but "himself":

"He that loveth his wife loveth himself. For no man ever yet hated his own flesh; but nourisheth and cherisheth it, even as the Lord the Church: for we are members of His body" (28b-30).

This startling reasoning, nevertheless sound and Scriptural, is based upon two facts:

(1) The identification of the woman with the man in her origin and nature. The story is told in Gen. 2:21-23:

"And the Lord God caused a deep sleep to fall upon Adam, and he slept; and He took one of his ribs, and closed up the flesh instead thereof. And the rib, which the Lord God had taken from man, made He a woman, and brought her unto the man. And Adam said, This is now bone of my bones, and flesh of my flesh: she shall be called Woman, because she was taken out of man."

This is the divine, immutable basis for marriage. From it marriage derives its mutual obligations. The wife is "the body" of the husband—the position of submission. But she is also "his own flesh"—let the husband love her as "himself."

(2) The identification of the Church with Christ in her origin and nature. The story is the same. In the death of Christ, our Adam, of which the first Adam's sleep was a type, His side too was opened. From it came "blood and water" (John 19:34), signifying in turn another "Body," deriving its life and nature from Him through His death (blood) and imparted Spirit of life (water). This, "His Body," was brought into being at Pentecost. It is so related to Him, its Head, as to be the counterpart of the wife in her original, derived relationship to the husband.

THE SACRED IMPLICATIONS OF CHRISTIAN MARRIAGE naturally follow (5:31-33). They are:

(1) Marriage is an intimate, indissoluble union (31). Necessarily so in its origin and nature. The two are "one flesh." It must supersede and supplant every other

relationship.   God so declared from the beginning: "Therefore shall a man leave his father and his mother, and shall cleave unto his wife: and they shall be one flesh" (Gen. 2:24).   So the Son of God, to woo and claim His Bride, left His Father and His Father's house.

(2) The Christian is bound to hold marriage sacred and indissoluble since it mirrors forth the mystery of Christ and His Church (32):

"This is a great mystery: but I speak concerning Christ and the Church."

Can Christ cast off His Church?   Then may a man cast aside his wife.   Can the Church separate herself from Christ?   Then may the wife sever her relationship to her husband.   The bonds are of kindred nature and import.   The one, visible, on earth, pictures the other, invisible, consummated in heaven.   To violate the one is to do violence to the sacredness of the other.

"Love" and "Reverence" (33) are the essence of the mutual marriage obligations in the Lord.   Thus is it that wedded life, sanctified and sweetened by a sacred purpose, less sordid, more spiritual than physical, sets about fulfilling its heavenly mission on earth.

Comment

WOMAN'S POSITION is defined in Scripture with clarity and certainty.   Whatever she may be personally, positionally she is not above man, nor yet on a parity. This is the divine order: based upon her origin from man; disregarded in her acting independently of her "head" in the temptation (the woman was "deceived," not the man—1 Tim. 2:14) ; restored in Christ, our new spiritual Head, whose headship has been a blessing beyond all compare to womankind.   Were any one tempted to take exception to Scripture's teaching in the matter of woman's position, he should pause to consider that the same system of Christian teaching has elevated woman to a position incomparably above what she was, and still is, under non-Christian systems.

We live in a day of "woman's rights." Politically, and possibly in other spheres, when what she has gained is balanced by what she has lost, her advantage is in doubt. Woman's divinely ordered position, not her man-accorded privileges, is her place of power.

Spiritually, her disregard of the divine order spells chaos. Had she never stepped out from her position, as she did in the garden to listen to the lure of Satan inviting her to act independently of her head, we would not today have such religious perversions as Seventh Day Adventism, Christian Science, Theosophy, Pentecostalism, etc. Fully accepting the leadership of her Lord, woman has a golden opportunity, in gratitude for the position to which He has elevated her, to help restore the consciousness of His spiritual authority in and through the Church.

Marriage That Sticks. A day of easy divorce has lowered marriage to a level little above a civil contract, terminable at will. The havoc is appalling. Truancy and kindred problems come from broken homes. The moral waste and wreckage are appalling. God's people are largely accountable. The increasing rupture of home ties has merely paralleled and kept pace with a corresponding unfaithfulness toward Christ in the Church. Spiritual harlotry is rife. Few in the Church care that they are "married to another, even to Christ." Here is to be found the antidote for the divorce mill. Let Christians regard with renewed sacredness their union with Christ, living in utter faithfulness to the heavenly home ties, and we may expect to see that faithfulness reflected in the earthly marriage bond. But not

till then: God has too much regard for the flouted love
of His Son.

BACK TO BEGINNINGS. It is little wonder that Satan
hates the opening chapters of Genesis and has inspired
effort toward their discrediting. Our modern problems present a new reason for getting back to their
authoritative account of origins. Adrift on the open
sea of speculation and experimentation, the sanctions
of marriage there found alone will suffice. To know
that we are one, not in our personal marriage venture
but in the beginning, in our origin, in the unchangeable nature of things—this will restore marriage to its
rightful sanctity and inviolability. Likewise the
Church. To know that she came from the side of
Christ, owes her very existence to Him in such an intimate source of life as to be "of His flesh and of His
bones"—knowing this, how can we cut the life-cord,
steal her from Him and, ignoring His right in her and
headship over her, devote her to the teachings of men,
to activities and aims wholly foreign to her calling and
equally repugnant to Him? Back to the beginning, in
creation, in redemption—this will guide and counsel
us to the right ending.

2—As Children and Parents, We Are Children of Our Heavenly Father, 6:1-4

Note

CHILDREN TO OBEY THEIR PARENTS (6:1-3). We
have reached the second relationship of the family, the
fruit and purposed outcome of the wife and husband relationship. As wives were mentioned first, so now the
children; and for the same reason. Children represent
the side of human responsibility in this earthly reflection of the heavenly family: together we are children

to Him who is our Father. The duty resting upon children in the family is that they "obey."

THE MANNER of obedience (1b) is "in the Lord." To fit into this requirement children must needs *be* in the Lord before they can *obey* in the Lord. Yet all children are under obligation to the universal law of parenthood. "In the Lord" can scarcely be limited to the will of Christ, for that would suggest a discernment they might not possess; rather, in the spirit of being pleasing to Him in the matter of filial obedience. Happy the children with such home requirements.

THE REASON for obedience (1c). In one word: it is "right." The child has been ushered into a world regulated by the law of obedience. The heavenly bodies, the seasons, the vegetable kingdom, the animal kingdom—all are under its sway. The heart, the family, the Church, the State are the spheres of man's obedience. God requires it throughout life: He places the child in the home, there to learn the rightfulness of it.

FIRST COMMANDMENT WITH PROMISE (2, 3). The duty of obedience is enjoined by appeal to the command: "Honour thy father and thy mother" which is cited as "the first commandment with promise." God wrote this duty into the decalogue, so fundamental is it to His economy, and graciously added a promise of blessing, which the Spirit here writes over into the New Covenant.

DUTY OF PARENTS TO CHILDREN (6:4). In using the word *fathers* there is no thought of taking responsibility for the children from the mother. It is a term for parenthood. Doubtless the word *father* is designed to remind us that we stand to our children as our Heavenly Father does to us. The parent's duty is stated negatively and positively:

(1) Not to incite to anger by a severity of treatment that arouses resentment and robs of respect for parental authority when not exercised with restraint.

(2) Rather, to nurture them, everything that is conducive to their growth and development in the continuous process of child-training, for such is the meaning of the word, educating, culturing, disciplining. To this is to be added admonition, literally, *laying before the mind,* instruction in the things of the Lord, the inculcating of His precepts, the guiding of the young feet into His ways.

Well may we recall, as a pattern for Christian parents, the direction given to Jewish home-makers:

"And these words, which I command thee this day, shall be in thine heart: and thou shalt teach them diligently unto thy children, and shalt talk of them when thou sittest in thine house, and when thou walkest by the way, and when thou liest down, and when thou risest up. And thou shalt bind them for a sign upon thine hand, and they shall be as frontlets between thine eyes. And thou shalt write them upon the posts of thy house, and on thy gates" (Deut. 6:6-9).

Comment

GIVE THE CHILDREN A CHANCE. This is but another way of saying: Give God a chance with the children. This, in turn, means in our day: Save our country by saving the home. Never were there so many enemies of the home, so many forces at work to empty it of meaning and rob it of character-forming qualities. So much is "sent out." And we "go out," if not for our meals, at least for our good times. We trust our children to agencies, outside of the home. Will they inculcate the fear of God, a saving knowledge of Christ? God holds parents responsible for the life they have brought into the world. We must study to make our home-life tell for Him.

CHRISTIAN PARENTAGE. Our children had not the

chance to choose their parents; we should see to it that they have the best. We have the making and shaping of their lives so largely in our hands. Are they not entitled to a Christian up-bringing? Any other inheritance, however generous, is a poor substitution. We recall one earnest mother saying to us, when pressed for a decision for Christ: "If ever I feel the need of being a Christian, it is when I think of my children and my responsibility to them."

"FORTY YEARS TOO LATE." A young man, consulting a physician as to his condition, was told by him: "You should have come to me forty years ago." "Why," said the young man, "I am only twenty-five years old." "Yes, I know," said the physician, "your father should have consulted me fifteen years before you were born." O the responsibilities of parenthood! The handicaps of life are many: shall we load them onto our children? Or shall we lift them by truly Christian living and truly Christian training in a truly Christian home?

3—As Servants and Masters We Serve Our Lord and Master, 6:5-9

Note

Again, as in the preceding, the duties involved in the relationship are set forth as to the *manner* of their performing and the *reason* therefor.

SERVANTS ARE TO BE OBEDIENT (6:5-8). In view of the fact that servants in the Orient, while counted a part of the household, were virtually slaves (the word throughout the New Testament is *doulos,* slave), some have argued that Christianity here places its approval upon slavery. Quite the contrary is the case. The teaching here given virtually lifts him out of his slavery and sets him free with a great freedom, of spirit if not of body. The bodily emancipation has since followed.

THE MANNER: "As unto the Lord" (6:5b-7). After reminding them that masters, such as they serve, are only such "according to the flesh," phrase is piled upon phrase for the securing of the finest type of service; three times being brought back to the one great liberating fact that they are servants of Christ: "with fear and trembling, in singleness of your heart, *as unto Christ.* Not with eyeservice, as men-pleasers; but *as the servants of Christ,* doing the will of God from the heart. With good will doing service, *as to the Lord, and not to men.*"

We are all servants, in some capacity, in various relationships. Some of us serve under a rigid severity of circumstances, some under a system that grinds us down. But here is teaching that lifts us up above our circumstances. The most menial routine of drudgery may be done, yes, must be done, "as unto the Lord." Indeed we are enjoined not to do it otherwise: "Not with eyeservice, as men-pleasers . . . as to the Lord, and *not* to men."

THE REASON (6:8) is a cogent one, carrying us over into the realm of future reward. Listen! "Knowing that whatsover good thing any man doeth," i.e., in the manner prescribed, as unto the Lord, which alone makes it good in His sight, "the same shall he receive again from the Lord." The teaching is twofold: 1— The Lord keeps a careful account of all service rendered as unto Him. 2—He is a faithful paymaster; nothing done for Him shall go unrewarded. Herein is the Scriptural spur and incentive to Christian service, in all spheres of life, though it go unrecognized and unrewarded of men. It opens the whole theme of Rewards, of which we shall have more in a moment.

MASTERS TOWARD THEIR SERVANTS (6:9). The matter is quickly disposed of, since the same principles are to govern here. THE MANNER of their treatment: "Do the same things, forbearing threatening." THE REASON: They, the masters of earth, have a Master in heaven who is Master of both and is no respecter of persons. He knows no class distinctions. He judges all by the same impartial standards of service.

Comment

THE SOLUTION OF INDUSTRIAL PROBLEMS is enshrined in these few verses. Self-interest tends to pit the employed against the employer and vice versa. But consider how each would look upon the things of the other were this teaching to govern their relationship. Many times the employer is overexacting and overbearing, rather than "forbearing"; at times the employed careless and listless, with no heart in his work. Take a factory of a thousand men: what would be the transformation in spirit and output were the thousand to come to their benches or machines purposing that the day's work should express their earnest, heartfelt desire to serve the Lord, out of gratitude to Him? The result, from every imaginable angle, would be amazing. Pity is that men are not prepared to make the demonstration. Yet God's child can have the joy of it every day that he toils.

OUR UNCOLLECTED WAGES. The Apostle's declaration that we shall receive again from the Lord what we have rendered of service as unto Him reminds us of his word of confidence in the face of every present disappointment and deprivation: "For the which cause I also suffer these things: nevertheless I am not ashamed: for I know whom I have believed, and am persuaded that

He is able to keep that which I have committed unto Him against that day" (2 Tim. 1:12).

Doubtless he had in mind the custom in the Roman army whereby a soldier might leave his wages to accumulate with the paymaster. His bed and board being found, why should he collect more than a portion for his present needs? Then, one day, his service ended, in taking his discharge he is surprised at the amount coming to him. How welcome for establishing the home of which he has dreamed!

How eager should we be for service that gives opportunity for laying up wages with Him! How glad when we have rendered service that men failed to know, to note, or to reward. He knows and is holding it for the great pay-day.

THE MOTIVE OF SERVICE, then, is what counts with our Lord. How can we miss this when we recall His familiar words of Matt. 6:1-18, R.V. "Take heed that ye do not your righteousness before men, to be seen of them: else ye have no reward with your Father who is in heaven" (vs. 1). Note the warning: *"No* reward *with* your Father." Certainly not. You did it to be seen of men, hoping to get from them what they thought you deserved! You cannot expect to be paid twice. You have no claim on the One in whose service you were not consciously engaging.

Then our Lord cites three spheres of service, giving, praying, fasting, in order that He may enforce His opening declaration by the threefold warning: "Verily I say unto you, They have their reward. . . . They have their reward. . . . They have their reward" (vv. 2, 5, 16) ; accompanied by a threefold commendation for the *right* way of doing the same thing, "In secret: and Thy Father who seeth in secret shall recompense thee. . . .

Shall recompense thee. . . . Shall recompense thee"
(vv. 4, 6, 18).

What a challenge! Would you prefer your pay now,
passing, from men, with nothing from Him? Or
would you prefer to go on, unwearied, seeking nothing
from men, that you may have it then, fadeless, from
Him? Your answer will be in the *motive* of service,
determining its *manner*. The answer will enrich or
impoverish eternity for you.

THE SPUR TO SERVICE. How much this teaching is
needed in a day of superficial and man-made methods
to maintain good works in the face of flagging energies.
In securing the church budget, so-and-so could scarcely
be expected to give his hundreds unless means were at
hand of letting folks know how generous a giver he is.
What benefactions would never happen, what community drives would fail, were the principle of secrecy,
"as unto the Lord," maintained in them.

On the other hand, how many dear people of God
are fainting in their service because men are slow to
approve or slightly applaud. Stung to inaction by the
sense of ingratitude! We all need to turn often to
these Scriptures to nerve us to renewed service. Men
require a sense of reward, somehow, somewhere. We
have it, fully assured, from Him and in Him. Beyond
all that He may give us will be Himself. Anticipating
the sight of His face then, we need to *see* Him now, as
the antidote to faintness and weariness, the sufficient
spur to untiring service.

The Bride-to-Be

Reference to the *chart* shows this to be the appeal to
which we must revert. Believers are constituted His
Body, His Building, His Bride. All that the Church

now is, by way of privilege or duty, leads to the cul-
minating relationship of Bride to the Bridegroom.
Hence the emphasis in this family treatise, overshadowing all else, is upon wives and husbands. The reason, as the Apostle explains, is that he is using it to
elucidate to us "a great mystery," even that of "Christ
and the Church."

This brings us into the realm of love; unalloyed love;
love that moulds and fashions life: love that determines
conduct; love that never fails; His love to us and its
reflection in our love to Him—the love that secured
to us our Standing and that in turn assures our Walking in conformity thereto.

Consider what this love, His and ours from Him,
does:

(1) Love Covers. It "covers" our sin in the Atonement, for this is the manner of God's dealing with it
in blood-redemption. In the Old Testament we read:
"Love covereth all sin" (Prov. 10:12). In the New
Testament: "Love covereth a multitude of sins" (1 Pet.
4:8, R.V.). Again, "Love beareth all things" (1 Cor.
13:7) says in the original, "Love covers over all
things."

His love has treated us thus. Of His perverse people
it is said: "He hath *not beheld* iniquity in Jacob"
(Num. 23:21). Lot, mixing in with Sodom, made a
miserable failure of his life. Yet the New Covenant
says nothing of it, not a word; rather, it calls him
"righteous Lot." Ah, yes, love covers. David sinned
heinously, unspeakably. Yet in the experience of God's
love he cried: "Blessed is he whose transgression is forgiven, whose sin is covered" (Ps. 32:1). Did it cover?
In the New Covenant, with repeated reference to
David, there is not a single intimation of his sin. He is
the man after God's own heart. How wondrously love

covers. It is the glory of the Gospel of Grace.

Human love, genuine love, behaves the same. Does the mother, when her boy has outraged the proprieties with some evil word or deed, proceed to tell it abroad, or even whisper it about? No, indeed. She holds it in silence, for *love covers.*

Doubtless He is waiting for His love to behave the same, through us, in all household affairs, earthly and heavenly. What new endearments would characterize the home ties. How fine the fellowship in the church where unkindly criticism comes to be strangely absent because love keeps covering.

(2) LOVE SEPARATES. Lover's love means utter separation. Its culmination in the marriage bond rests upon separation: "Forsaking all others, cleave lovingly to him—to her—as long as we both do live." We are unworthy of His love, having such a marriage scene in anticipation, when we refuse to bring to its altar of daily devotion the same mindedness.

In all the earth there is nothing more beautiful than a maiden, who, having yielded to the wooings of a lover, moves in and out among her fellows with that quiet reserve that is bred of the consciousness that she belongs to another and that one day he will claim her as his own. Without holding herself aloof, there is always in her bearing and conduct that which brings to mind this unseen bond and begets respect for it.

It is this that Christ asks and expects of His Church —a love that separates; a separation that casts a charm about the anticipated culmination of our love affair; a bearing of quiet reserve such as will suffice to remind all about us that we belong to Him. He is not content, nor should we be, with anything less.

(3) LOVE PERFECTS. His love always has a goal in

view. What He purposes He has only revealed in part.
This we know that He plans to present us to Himself
in a degree of perfection that is not marred by "spot
or wrinkle or any such thing." The way it will come
about? Well, we are going to see Him, no longer
darkly or dimly, but face to face. The sight will be
transforming: "We shall be like Him, for we shall
see Him as He is."

The story is told of a certain maiden, betrothed to a
man across the sea. The day was set and a resplendent
church wedding planned. But she was blind. A spe-
cialist, learning the circumstances, asked the privilege
of examining her eyes, gave his opinion that she might
possibly see, then declared his willingness to operate.
He imposed the one condition that the bandages be
removed from her hitherto sightless eyes by the bridegroom himself. It was done. The day came. The
bridal party met at the altar. Then, in the presence of
all, with his own hands, the bridegroom from afar
undid the bandages with expectant hands. The result
—light came; sight came; for the first time she saw
and the sight that filled her eyes was her lover's face.

> The bride eyes not her garment,
>   But her dear bridegroom's face;
> I will not gaze at glory,
>   But on my King of grace,—
> Not at the crown He giveth,
>   But on His pierced Hand.
> The Lamb is all the glory
>   Of Immanuel's land.—*A. R. Cousin.*

CHAPTER VI

THE MOST WONDERFUL WARFARE
EVER WAGED

EPHESIANS 6:10-24

With the transition to this last word of Ephesians the Christian's Walk merges into a Warfare. Doubtless, at first thought, there is no little feeling of disappointment at such a conclusion. Why, we ask, must an Epistle of so high and lofty truth descend to a battlefield for its finale? Did not Christ win the victory? Are we not victorious in Him? Yea, as we have learned, already seated with Him in the heavenlies? May not our walk in Him continue on into the glory, into His own immediate presence?

Our questioning brings forth at least three evident reasons why the Christian pilgrim must also be the soldier of Christ, as he walks, prepared also to war. They are: Personal; Positional; Dispensational.

(1) THE PERSONAL REASON. We, as believers, have a traitor in the camp, the mind of the flesh, warring with our members, restless under the restraints the Spirit places upon him, ever desirous to take us out from the liberty of the sons of God and deliver us again into captivity to the bondage of the flesh and its lusts. Moreover, Satan has never given over his desire to "have" us. As the enemy of souls, envious of our salvation in Christ and allegiance to Christ, he is ceaselessly, actively, on the warpath, trailing the saints. Listen:

151

"Be sober, be vigilant; because your adversary the devil, as a roaring lion, walketh about, seeking whom he may devour: whom resist steadfast in the faith, knowing that the same afflictions are accomplished in your brethren that are in the world" (1 Pet. 5:8, 9).

(2) The Positional Reason. We, with all believers, are "the body of Christ." What does that mean to Satan? Just this—a signal for hostilities. When the Son of God took to Himself a body, Satan well knew His purpose through it to redeem the race. Through Herod he sought to destroy it. In the temptation he withstood it. Leaving him "for a season" only, he returned to dog His steps, to fire men's hearts with enmity against Him, till finally he saw the precious body on the cross, gripped in death.

Today that body, raised of God, is in the glory, above the power of Satan to touch it. But the Son of God is there as the Head of another body, His Church. This body is on earth, within the reach of Satan, and its identification with Christ draws to it the fire of the Adversary's hostility. Hence the persecutions following Pentecost, when the Spirit formed believers into this body, and down through the centuries. The reason is not personal but positional; we are the tangible portion of the personality of Christ—His body. So Jesus, looking prophetically down the centuries, warned: "If they do these things in a green tree, what shall be done in the dry?" (Luke 23:31).

(3) The Dispensational Reason. The word "dispensation," prominent in Ephesians, has to do with the divine "economy," God's arrangement, provision, plan, unfolding through the ages. It includes a revealed purpose to rule the world in righteousness by Jesus Christ. This means a final reckoning with the powers of evil and their ultimate dissolution. This necessitates a conflict, decisive and conclusive, between Christ and His

own, sharers with Him of His right to reign, and Satan and his own, pretenders to world-power and false claimants thereto. Satan, well aware of this inevitable closing in upon him and his power, undoubtedly is ordering much of his present-day strategies with this in view. John discerned in his own day that "the mystery of iniquity is already working" (1 John 4:3). The stage has long been set, and Christians of every age are a part of the preliminary skirmishings, bringing us nearer and nearer to the final conflict. Something of this enters into Paul's constraint to say a final word concerning warfare.

Outline

VI. Our Fighting Against Spiritual Foes Calls for Spiritual Weapons for the Conflict, 6:10-20.

    1. Our Strength for the Conflict—"Be Strong in the Lord," 6:10.

    Our Power must be "His might" (10a).

    2. Our Equipment for the Conflict—The Armour Provided of God, 6:11-17.

      a. The nature of the warfare (11b, 12).

      b. Makes needful the whole armour of God (13).

      c. Exhortation to put on the armour (14-17). For the Body—the Girdle of Truth; the Breastplate of Righteousness (14). For the Feet—the Gospel of Peace (15). For the Hand—the Shield of Faith (16). For the Head—the Helmet of Salvation (17a). For the Mouth—the Sword of the Spirit (the Word of God) (17b).

3. **Our "All Prayer" in the Conflict—Praying Always in the Spirit, 6:18-20.**
   a. The manner of praying (18a).
      (1) Always.
      (2) With all prayer and supplication.
      (3) In the Spirit.
      (4) Watching with all perseverance and supplication.
   b. The persons to be prayed for (18b-20).
      (1) For all saints (18b).
      (2) For the ministry (19, 20).
          Paul personally craves this help to boldness of utterance (19), particularly as he is an ambassador in bonds (20).

The Conclusion, 6:21-24.
   a. Personal greetings (21, 22).
   b. Parting salutation (23).
   c. Benediction (24).

Chart—see opposite page.

FINALLY VS. FOES sets forth the inevitableness of warfare with existing spiritual enemies.

CHRIST, GOD, SPIRIT are again the outstanding feature; the Trinity of God, the practical and sufficient provision for victory in the conflict.

ARMOUR, be it noted, is for the body; thus the conception of Christian living so fundamental to Ephesians, is carried out in this section also.

INWARD, OUTWARD, UPWARD is again the progress of thought to be kept in mind as the section unfolds. Our Strength is Inward; our Equipment is Outward; our Appeal is Upward.

PEACE AND GRACE sum up the believer's experience even in the midst of conflict.

Ephesians — HIS VERY OWN

	STAND-ING			WALK-ING		WAR-ING
	CHAP. 1	**CHAP. 2**	**CHAP. 3**	**4:1-5:20**	**5:21-6:9**	**6:10-24**
	AS HIS **BELIEVERS**	AS HIS **BODY** 1:22-23	AS HIS **BUILDING** 2:19-22	**WORTHILY** AS A BODY	**HEAVENLY** AS A FAMILY	**FINALLY** vs. FOES
Row 1	**FATHER** { CHOSE ADOPTS WILL ACCEPT 1:3-6	**QUICKENED** BY THE GRACE of **GOD** 2:1-10	**HOUSEHOLD** OF **GOD** 3:1-13 [MYSTERY OF MYSTERIES OF THE AGES]	**ONE BODY** (INWARD) STATURE of **CHRIST** 4:1-16	**WIVES** AND **HUSBANDS** 5:22-33	**STRENGTH** (INWARD) IN **CHRIST** 6:10
Row 2	**SON** { PURCHASED ENLIGHTENS WILL INHERIT 1:7-12	**MADE ONE** BY THE **BLOOD** OF **CHRIST** 2:11-17	**TEMPLE** IN THE **LORD** 3:6 [PARTITIONS REMOVED]	**NEW MAN** (OUTWARD) FRUIT of **SPIRIT** 4:17-32	**CHILDREN** AND **PARENTS** 6:1-4	**ARMOUR** (OUTWARD) OF **GOD** 6:11-17
Row 3	**SPIRIT** { SAVED SEALS WILL CLAIM 1:13,14	**ACCESS** BY THE **ONE SPIRIT** 2:18	**HABITATION** IN THE **SPIRIT** 3:14-21 [FILLED WITH GLORY]	**IN LOVE** (UPWARD) IMITATORS of **GOD** 5:1-20	**SERVANTS** AND **MASTERS** 6:5-9	**PETITION** (UPWARD) IN THE **SPIRIT** 6:18-20
Bottom	**P**rayer for **R**evelation / **P**ower of **R**esurrection	HE - Our Peace / WE - Fellowcitizens	**A**ble Exceeding **A**bundantly Above all we ask AMEN	Gifts of CHRIST / Graces of SPIRIT / Glory of GOD	**B**RIDE- TO-BE 5:31,32	**P**EACE and **P**GRACE AMEN

IN HIM - Our Standing in Heaven   IN US - His Walking on Earth

Amen is in counterposition with the Amen of the doctrinal part. All that is there of privileged position in Him—Amen; let it be realized by practical appropriation in us—Amen.

1—Our Strength for the Conflict—Strong in the Might of the Lord, 6:10

Note

"Finally," in the Greek, is not essentially a time word. Rather, "as for what remains to be said." Paul cannot leave these lofty truths with them under any misapprehension that "walking" is the sum of Christian conduct. They must be fully prepared for warfare.

"My Brethren." In the limited sense, of a common Father. In the wider sense, brothers together in a common cause. Soldiers are brothers in arms.

"Be Strong in the Lord." Not "from" the Lord, but first of all, "in" the Lord. Strong in the position which is ours in Him, just as the hand or foot has its strength in the body to which it belongs. "I can," says Paul, "do all things in Him that strengtheneth me" (Phil. 4:13). Thus, the *strength* that is ours for the conflict is "the *power* of His *might*" (three different Greek words).

But, be it noted, our strength is "in the Lord." In Ephesians the phrase is almost uniformly, "in Christ." The change here is significant. Indeed, the component parts of the full name *Jesus Christ our Lord* are used with marked discrimination.* Jesus, His personal, human name—He is our Saviour (Matt. 1:23); Christ, His official, mediatorial name—by Him we are indwelt (Gal. 2:20); Lord, His family, deity name—He is now

---

* The reader is referred to our book on Romans, *His Salvation*, page 139ff.

our Master (John 13:13) and is coming as Lord over all (Rev. 19:16).

Here, then, we are bidden to be strong in our victorious Lord, He who gained the victory for us and is coming to complete it in ultimate triumph. In the interim we are to triumph in Him. For example: "Sin shall not have dominion over you" (Rom. 6:14); the word in the Greek is *lord*. Sin shall not lord it over you; for sin is vanquished and Another is now your Lord.

Comment

No SUBSTITUTE can be found for the strength, might, power which comes from our position in Christ and His personal indwelling of us. Human personality is frail and faltering without it. Much in secular warfare has been made of "the man behind the guns." The Christian warrior is made fit with inner strength before ever the outwardness of equipment can profit him. Against Goliath, Saul's armour advantaged him nothing. He was inwardly weak and cowardly. A David could assay the battle because he was "strong in the Lord." The crying need of our day is for strong men. Let them go apart, know the Lord, permit Him to "clothe Himself" with them, then come forth to lead us to victory in the crucial conflicts of the hour.

2—Our Equipment for the Conflict—The Armour Provided by God, 6:11-17

Note

"PUT ON" (11a) transfers our concern at once to the external sphere. It brings "the body" once more to full consciousness. In Chapter 5 we were to put on clothing suited to the new man, moving in society. Here we are to put on armour necessary to the soldier, the man marching to war.

"The Whole Armour of God" (11b), a phrase that conveys both its origin and nature. It is of God's providing. It is also divinely adapted and made sufficient to our need; namely, that we "may be able to stand against the wiles of the devil." The Greek contains a play on words that is completely lost in translation: we are given the *panoplia* of God against the *methodia* of Satan. That is, Satan is full of "methods" which he adopts to outwit God, His plans and His people. Against these methods God has provided a "panoply," fully adapted to coping with them—He asks us to *put* it on, and *keep* it on.

The Spirit first sets before us Satan and his methods, indicating the nature of our warfare, that we may appreciate the necessity for such an armour as God has provided.

The Person, Position, Purpose, Power of the Enemy (11c, 12). Let us note carefully what is revealed concerning him and the hosts at his command: "That ye may be able to stand against the wiles of the devil. For our wrestling is not against flesh and blood, but against principalities, against the powers, against the worldrulers of this darkness, against the spiritual hosts of wickedness in the heavenly places" (11c. 12, R.V.).

We are not to deceive ourselves by thinking of the enemy as our equals, on our level, of the same order of being. No; "our wrestling is not against flesh and blood." Carnal weapons are of no avail in this warfare. Though we invent weapons galore, and though we do our utmost with them, still the enemy remains unscathed by them.

Who, then, are our enemies? Where are they? And what is their purpose and power?

(1) "The Devil." His person and position are revealed in the following designations: "The prince of this world" (John 12:31)—claimant to its throne. "The god of this age" (2 Cor. 4:4)—claiming and accepting its worship. "The prince of the power of the air" (Eph. 2:2)—exercising authority in the reaches of air above man's earth-level. Other descriptive titles: "The great dragon"; "that old serpent"; "the Devil"; "Satan"; "deceiveth the whole world" (Rev. 12:9—note also "his angels").

Of this majestic person, Scripture has considerable to say as regards his methods, reflecting the animus of his activities. We cite only the following: 2 Cor. 4:4— He blinds men's eyes to the Gospel. He achieves his ends by keeping souls in the dark, away from the "Light of the world." 2 Cor. 11:13-15—He transforms himself into an angel of light, standing in pulpits, impersonated in "ministers of righteousness" who leave the Gospel of salvation unheralded. Eph. 2:2—He is the spirit energizing men in their state of disobedience to God. Rev. 12:10—He accuses the brethren (and they surely give him material for framing his accusations). Rev. 12:9—He deceives men, even "the whole world."

Then, to these methods Satan adds that of *organization*. He fights not single-handed, but rules over a highly-organized empire.

(2) Satan's "Spiritual Hosts," which are organized into "principalities" and "powers," which constitute the "rulers of the darkness of this world," and are "in the heavenlies." However forbidding this array may seem, showing the sphere of satanic sway, this latter state-

ment as to their exalted position is calculated to startle us. It ties this section in with all that goes before, being one of the key expressions of Ephesians. Christ is in the heavenlies. In Him we are seated there. A glorious triumph, it seemed. But now we are told there in the heavenlies Satan has his abode and base of operations. How disconcerting!

Thank God, there are three heavens (2 Cor. 12:2): the atmospheric heavens; the starry heavens; the heaven of heavens. In this last are "our Father's house" and throne; Christ is seated there. From it Satan is excluded. He was there in his perfection, until the sin of pride seized him (Ezek. 28:14, 15; Isa. 14:13, 14). Now limited to the second heaven and "the power of the air," he will soon, with his angels, be "cast down" to the earth-level (Rev. 12:7-12). This "war" in heaven is the opening of the last war of this age: it becomes conclusive, eventuating in the casting of Satan and his henchmen into the bottomless pit (Rev. 19:20; 20:2, 3).

"WHEREFORE TAKE THE WHOLE ARMOUR OF GOD" (13). How cogent is the "therefore." The necessity for so doing is perfectly evident to all, if the above be true. "Take," not "make." There is a world of difference. Man's attempts to make an armour are pitiful and foolhardy. God has made it, in the perfection of His redemptive grace; we have but to "take" it to ourselves. It is thus that we shall "be able to *stand against* in the evil day, and having done all, to stand."

The "evil day" that may overtake us, whether of sickness, poverty, persecution, temptation or testing of whatever sort, is but a type and anticipation of the ultimate "evil day" that draws on apace as the world-conflict closes in (Rev. 19:11ff).

THE WHOLE ARMOUR, EVERY PIECE IN PLACE (14-

17). God's Word is wonderful for the absence of abstractions. It refuses to deal with them. The Armour is not put on display. We are not even told of what it consists until we see it actually in place, each piece as designed, covering and caring for the whole body.

The Whole Armour	The Whole Body
Girdle of Truth ⎫ Breastplate of Righteousness ⎭	The Body (14)
Shoes—the Gospel of Peace	The Feet (15)
Shield of Faith	The Hand (16)
Helmet of Salvation	The Head (17a)
Sword of the Spirit	The Mouth (17b)

The Girdle of Truth for the loins. While the girdle was often studded with gems to make it beautiful—and truth is always that—its purpose was far more than ornamental. It was most essential to the wrestler, upgirding and lending strength to his vitals. The man who loves the truth and lives it, this man is indeed girded with strength.

The Breastplate of Righteousness. For the protection of the most vulnerable parts, his vital organs, the heart and lungs, where a wound would prove fatal —for this nothing short of righteousness will suffice. Of our God we read: "He put on righteousness as a breastplate" (Isa. 49:7). Elsewhere Paul urges "putting on the breastplate of faith and love" (1 Thess. 5: 8). Faith is merely that by which we acquire righteousness (Rom. 4:5). God's righteousness alone is woundproof but it must be so "put on" as to become our own —righteousness imputed by faith and imparted by love.

The Gospel of Peace upon the Feet. It is spoken of as a "preparation," that is, an experience of the good news of peace that imparts readiness for every hardship, for every rough place in the pathway. Placed upon his feet it enables him to overcome the world wherever he makes contact with it—see Jesus' words in John 16:33. As the Persian proverb has it, "To him who wears shoes, the whole earth is covered with leather." Such an experience is, in turn, a "preparation" to minister to others: "As it is written, How beautiful are the feet of them that preach the gospel of peace, and bring glad tidings of good things" (Rom. 10:15).

The Shield of Faith for the Hand. "Above all," that is, of importance as an element of equipment beyond all that has been enjoined. The reason is added in the fact that the enemy uses not merely weapons that cut and thrust but those that fly through the air, darts that are aflame with the poison of his own evil passions. But they are of power, these temptations and suggestions, only as they penetrate our person: they must be "quenched" before they reach us. The hand must be furnished with a protector for the body, serving the purpose of the large shield, carried by the Roman soldier.

The quality of the Christian's shield is "faith." We recall how frequently and variously the Old Testament refers to "God our shield" (Gen. 15:1; 2 Sam. 22:3; Ps. 84:9, 11; etc.). Faith is that whereby we appropriate Him and make Him ours; and, confessedly, Satan's darts can have no possible effect upon Him.

The Helmet of Salvation for the Head. Elsewhere Paul's phrasing is, "for an helmet the hope of salvation." This suggests salvation in its future aspect, that the helmeting of the head is with the prospect and anticipation of salvation. Yet the distinction is scarcely to be drawn, for the hope of future salvation rests upon the assurance of present salvation. What we need is the knowledge of salvation as an assured, experimental fact. This constitutes the Christian's head-piece, the divine protection for the intellectual life. How greatly it is needed! The university life of today has produced any number of young people who, facing the intellectual problems of a skeptical age in their own fancied strength, have come to question the very existence of God. Having on the head-piece of salvation, the knowledge of the efficacy of God's saving grace, the entire process of one's thinking is shaped and safeguarded thereby.

THE SWORD OF THE SPIRIT for the Mouth. This is explained to be the Word of God, a term employed here of the Scriptures of truth finding oral expression through us. Two instances come to mind where the Word is referred to in a militant manner: "The Word of God is living, and active, and sharper than any two-edged sword, and piercing even to the dividing of soul and spirit, of both joints and marrow, and quick to discern the thoughts and intents of the heart' (Heb. 4:12, R.V.); again, speaking of our glorified Lord: "Out of His mouth went a sharp two-edged sword" (Rev. 1:16). Of the entire armour the sword is evidently the most spiritual and the most significant. The most spiritual in that, formed by the Spirit to convey the thought, and accomplish the purpose, of God in spiritual warfare, its wielding is merely the intelligence-laden breath of the believer—the human spirit voicing the divine Spirit. The most significant in that it is the only part of the panoply that can by any means play the part of offensive warfare (in reality it is defensive as well as offensive). Moreover, it calls for the greatest degree of devotion, since the mere repetition of words will not make them an efficient sword: spoken in the Spirit, out of a heart filled with the Spirit, they become indeed the effective sword of the Spirit.

Comment

THE PERSONALITY OF SATAN is an outstandingly revealed fact in the pages, and in the purpose, of God's Word, quite parallel to the personality of God Himself, until his final defeat is depicted. He speaks; he plans; he deceives; he hates; he plots; he fights—things that can be attributed only to personality. Yet hosts of people, despite this clear revelation, declare that they do not believe in a devil. The amazing thing is that some of them profess the utmost devotion to the truth of God's Word. It is certainly a tribute to Satan's success, for this is one of his "methods," to conceal his activities behind the smoke-screen of the persuasion that he does not exist.

A FALSE OPTIMISM rears it head wherever there is failure to recognize Satan as a chief factor in human affairs. Men think to bring in the millennium; yet Satan, with the hosts at his command, laughs at their efforts. Let them do their utmost, he ranges over his vast domains unhindered, plotting and planning at will. When will men realize that there is but one way to outdo him; namely, to take one's stand on the ground of Calvary, confronting him with the Cross where he became, and must ever continue to be, a defeated foe?

THE WHOLE BODY ARMOURED. Each piece of this wonderful panoply is available only to the one who comes to Calvary for it. Thus coming and "taking" it to himself, he has no excuse for any vulnerable spot— the whole body is covered. But hold—there is none for the back! No, there is no provision for Christian turning his back and running from the foe. The armour makes him "able to stand against" the enemy. So doing we are safe—and victorious.

DEFENSIVE RATHER THAN OFFENSIVE. It is significant that this entire equipment is defensive in character. While the Sword of the Spirit is of use for aggressive warfare, our Lord used it in a notable conflict to parry the thrusts of the adversary (Matt. 4:1-11). God has provided the armour primarily to protect the most precious thing He has on earth, the Body of His own Son. It is, so He says, that we "may be able to *stand against* in the evil day, and having done all, to *stand*." Stand! That is what He asks of us, meaning, stand as the victors that we are—*stand in the victory of Calvary*. It is the reiteration of Ephesian truth: we are in Christ; we stand victors in Him.

3—Our All-Prayer in the Conflict—Praying Always in the Spirit, 6:18-20

Note

THE PROVISION OF PRAYER is not to be regarded, along with the above, as a part of the equipment. Rather it takes us into the realm of the believer's resource, a resource of the Spirit, rendering the whole armour effective; only through prayer can we actually "take" it and "put it on," making it our very own in actual experience. Nor is it prayer for ourselves; rather, that the whole Body of Christ may be effectively panoplied.

THE ALLS OF PRAYER (18). The prayer to which we are exhorted is to be: 1—all sorts; 2—at all seasons; 3—for all saints; 4—with all steadfastness of spirit.

"All prayer" seems to refer to the varied elements that enter into true prayer, such as adoration, confes-

sion, thanksgiving, petition, intermingled with "sup-
plication," the earnest desire and pleading of the soul,
for the relief which it seeks. This is not to be inter-
mittent, but "always," springing from a fountain of
desire, welling up "in the Spirit," who is our prompter
to "pray without ceasing." Thus prayer is to find expression on all appropriate occasions, in the privacy of
our closet, in the family circle, in public gatherings of
believers, in the councils of the Church, in the unex-
pected emergency, in the unseen uplifting of the heart
while walking on the street or otherwise engaged. It
is to comprehend "all saints," all who are in Christ
Jesus, all who make up His Body, all who draw the
enmity of Satan, all for whom the armour has been
provided. Then, having made our petition, we are not
to forget it but to follow it with earnest, steadfast
watchfulness for its fulfillment.

PRAYER FOR THE PREACHER (19, 20). In particular,
prayer should be on behalf of that part of the Body
that has responsibility above the other members. The
Apostle lets it be known that he, so far from being
above the need of being prayed for, feels his utter de-
pendence upon their faithfulness in prayer for him,
believing that thereby he will be strengthened and emboldened in his gospel utterance. Regarding himself
as "an ambassador in bonds"—how admirably the
Apostle maintains the dignity of his calling!—he would
have them help in prayer to keep the gospel from being
bound.

Comment

PRAYER IN EPHESIANS reaches its pinnacle, the highest height it anywhere attains. Prayer is the appeal of
the believer, down here on the earth-level, to Him who

is in the highest heavens. By prayer we penetrate the furthest reaches of the enemy's domain, whatever "heavenlies" he may control, and lay claim to the resources of Him who is above them all. Whatever power the enemy possesses, before Him it is but weakness. Again, prayer in Ephesians is the occupation of the Body of Christ. It is coöperative, each member accepting prayer-responsibility on behalf of every other. Thus, when one discerns the mystical Body into which salvation has introduced him, he discovers that he has been inducted into a great world-wide union. His prayer-life is no longer self-centered, nor is it narrow in its sympathies. As in its upward reach it scales the heights of the heavenlies, so in its outward reach it comprehends the least and the greatest of the children of grace.

PRAYER TRANSFORMS PREACHERS. Many churches complain, and with sufficient reason, of the unscriptural and inefficient ministry from their pulpits; yet few accept seriously the means God has provided of changing their pastors into preachers of power. Modern unbelief need not be suffered in our pulpits if a believing pew set itself to pray. One instance is outstanding: Dr. R. A. Torrey, according to his own confession, was saturated when he entered the ministry with German rationalism. Two devoted women in his congregation, hearing his utterances, instead of harshly criticizing, sweetly remarked to him, "We are praying for you." Soon the change came—an utter revolution; and the world knows the result in a ministry devoted to the Word of God and the winning of souls. Other cases could be cited, involving changes markedly radical or more gradual, calculated to encourage God's people everywhere to claim a like prayer benefit.

THE GOSPEL MADE PLAIN. Paul asks for prayer enabling him to "make known the mystery of the gospel." Aside from the primary meaning of the phase, it must be confessed that the gospel is today, in its true intent, "hidden" from many people (2 Cor. 4:3, 4). Few people understand the Gospel, because it is seldom presented in its purity, as God's proposal of grace. O, for prayer-partners, petitioning that the gospel may be fully presented and as fully comprehended.

WATCH AND PRAY. Our warfare calls for those who will pray and "watch thereunto with all perseverance," not content to accept personal ease or prosperity while the cause of the Lord languishes and His people are supine before the foe. Well may we urge one another to renewed watchfulness as the price of victory.

> Christian, seek not yet repose;
> Cast thy dreams of ease away,
> Thou art in the midst of foes;
>   "Watch and pray."
>
> Principalities and powers,
> Mustering their unseen array,
> Wait for thine unguarded hours;
>   "Watch and pray."
>
> Gird thy heavenly armour on,
> Wear it ever night and day;
> Ambushed lies the Evil One:
>   "Watch and pray."
>
> Hear, above all, hear thy Lord,
> Him thou lovest to obey;
> Hide within thy heart His word,
>   "Watch and pray."
>
> Watch, as if on that alone
> Hung the issue of the day;
> Pray that help may be sent down:
>   "Watch and pray."

—Charlotte Elliott.

THE EPISTLE CONCLUDES (21-24) with the briefest possible personal reference by the Apostle, the briefer because he is commissioning Tychicus not only to carry the letter but particularly to tell them fully of his affairs, thus exhibiting a very tender regard for his readers in their affection for him, and a deep concern for their comfort and encouragement (21, 22).

Then follows a twofold benediction—to his immediate readers and to all who bear the name of Christ. To the Ephesians: "Peace be to the brethren, and love with faith, from God the Father and the Lord Jesus Christ" (23). To all believers: "Grace be with all them that love our Lord Jesus Christ in sincerity" (24).

This supernal epistle, opening with a salutation of "Grace and Peace," blesses those who have entered into its transforming truths with assurance of abiding "Peace and Grace."

The "Amen" of its lofty doctrines holds an answering "Amen" for all who prove its truths in practical devotion.

THE APPEAL

THE CHURCH OF CHRIST—*HIS VERY OWN*

While the foregoing is a studied attempt to discover the lofty teachings of Ephesians and the life that flows therefrom, the sore need of their application to the present day has been constantly in mind. In many quarters and on a number of counts the Church seems to be losing ground—thoughtful people fear for her. Why? We answer: Because the *invisible* Church has been lost to view. The Church of Ephesians is but little understood or considered; yet the Ephesian Church is the *real* Church.

In our day the Church is an *organization*. It is thought of and planned for in terms of officers and committees; secretaries and promoters; salaries and budgets; buildings and properties; problems and policies; methods to meet the problems and machinery to carry out the policies. Yet—not one of these, nor all of them combined, constitute the Church as we find it to be in Ephesians. None of them supplies the vital element that brings any group of people into the Church and her distinctive life.

Moreover, when men think thus of the Church, when the human element so evidently predominates that at times it seems to be her all, two things result: 1—Men lose their respect and rightful reverence for the Church. The mystical element is gone: they regard her and deal with her as with any other organization. 2—Men make bold to use her for ends extraneous to her charter. Formed for a purpose, that purpose is lightly brushed aside in zeal to have the Church occupy the largest possible place of service in the community.

But there is a principle at stake. It is this: *the valued things of life are reserved for a special purpose.* Let us see it through illustration. Here is a Rolls Royce car. Possessed of such evident power, why not set it to hauling sand and gravel? Again, it is so capacious; why not load it with delivery bundles? We are restrained from putting it to these uses by the fact that it is *reserved* for the uses for which, at great cost, it has been specially appointed. Yonder is a spacious dwelling. Just four people occupy it—what a waste! It would serve so well the social needs of the community. But no; serving such a purpose it cannot maintain the end for which it exists—it is *reserved* for the family.

Applying this principle to the Church—and it is assuredly among our most valued possessions—we recognize that the Church may readily be brought to defeat, simply through failure to keep her *reserved*-for-her, intended use. The purpose of Ephesians is to set before us this fact, that *the Church belongs to the Lord; that it is His Very Own; that He has reserved it to Himself for His designed and designated ends.*

His Very Own—By Name

The New Testament name for "church" is *ecclesia,* from which comes our word *ecclesiastical.* It means "the called out." Having to do with our calling, its consideration is deferred for the moment. In the providence and purpose of God the name used the world over has another derivation, of deep significance.

Twice in the New Testament occurs the word *kuriake,* derived from *kurios,* Lord; it means something "belonging to the Lord." 1—In 1 Cor. 11:20, of

"the Lord's Supper." It is a supper that belongs to
the Lord; it consists of His body and His blood; it is
so intimately His own that separated from Him it has
no meaning or existence. 2—In Rev. 1:10, of "the
Lord's day." The first day of the week is a day that
belongs to the Lord; on it He arose from the dead; on
it He poured forth His Spirit; it is a day that speaks
of Him, forever associated with Him, His worship,
His glory, in the minds and lives of His followers.

Similarly the word came to be applied to the Church.
Seizing upon the outstanding characteristic, it was said,
"Why, it is *kuriake,* something belonging to the Lord,
intimately and indissolubly associated with Him." And
that name has passed into practically all languages.
Note that the root letters are variably *krk, crc,* or
chrch. Here is a list: Anglo Saxon, *circe;* Dutch, *kerk;*
German, *kirche;* Norwegian, *kirke;* Swedish, *kyrka;*
Danish, *kirke;* Scotch, *kirk;* English, *church.*

Thus, dear reader, whenever you speak the name
"Church," you confess to this deep, abiding, intimate
and indissoluble association with the Lord. Are you
careful to see that this *belonging* is carried out with
honesty and consistency?

His Very Own—By Calling

If there is anything that should be self-evident regarding the Church it is that she has been "called" for
a specific and definite purpose, called to fill a place in
the divine economy that can be filled by no other
agency. This fact is embodied in the name He has
given her; it is designed to remind her, and all who
belong to her, that she is "called with a holy calling."

But the name states also the nature of the calling,
ecclesia, the called out. Called out from the mass of

THINKING THROUGH EPHESIANS

STANDING "IN CHRIST"			**I**
1	**2**	**3**	**DOCTRINAL**
BELIEVERS	**BODY**	**BUILDING**	
FATHER	**SON**	**SPIRIT**	Our
CHOSE in GRACE	BOUGHT with BLOOD	FILLS with LOVE	Standing In
Prayer for Fullness of Light		Prayer for Fullness of Love	Heaven— "In Him"
ABIDE "IN ME" (23 TIMES)		I "IN YOU" (4 TIMES) ★	
II **PRACTICAL**	**SURRENDER EVER** TO THE **SPIRIT**		**SURRENDER NEVER** TO **SATAN**
	4:1-5:21	5:22-6:9	6:10-24
His Walking On Earth— "In Us"	**BODY** of **CHRIST**	**BRIDE** of **CHRIST**	**SOLDIER** of **CHRIST**
	Worthy in our Walk	Set Apart by His LOVE	Stand in His Strength

★ *The Climax of Section I and transition to Section II is Paul's Prayer (3:14-21) "In Him" changes to "In Us." Ephesians = John 15 expanded under other imagery.*
I – *Christ the Vine: Our Position is "In Him."*
II – *We the Branches: His Fruit is "In Us."*

humanity, who have no relationship to Him, called into an intimacy with Himself such as would enable Him to mould and fashion her to His purposes. This out-calling He has secured and made effective in a threefold way. She is:

(1) His Very Own—Bought by His Blood. A transaction has taken place which is as binding as any "buy" effected by men. A price has been paid, hence, "Ye are not your own; ye are bought with a price." Have we made delivery—delivery of ourselves—to Him who in consequence is the owner? Further, we are blood-bought, which is much more than money-bought. My coat, mine merely by money, I can discard for another. Not so the blood-bought; it *belongs* —belongs to one's self.

(2) His Very Own—Baptized by His Spirit. This means His moving in to possess His property, to make it in truth His own. Baptized, as we are, into His body, we cease to be a bit of the common clay and become a part of His personality, His New Man, moulded into His image, made responsive to His will—His Spirit actuating our spirit.

(3) His Very Own—Sealed Unto Final Redemption. In the past, *purchased* by blood; for the present, *possessed* by His Spirit; for the future, *preserved* for the most glorious purposes ever conceived, surpassing the imagination of man, purposes which consummate upon His Church for the ages to come.

His Very Own—In Threefold Relationship

In Ephesians we are made to realize that our calling is to *be* something far more than to do something, and that the doing is the normal and natural expression of the being. Hence our threefold calling is embodied in a threefold relationship, wherein we are *His Very Own:*

(1) AS THE BODY BELONGS TO THE HEAD. How intimate! How responsive! If the body did not do, instantly and instinctively, the bidding of the head, it would be such an unwonted experience as to cause consternation—we would consult a physician at once. The hand picks up the book, the foot moves forward, seemingly anticipating the will of the head. So has He chosen His own to be to Him.

(2) AS THE BUILDING BELONGS TO THE FOUNDATION. The correspondence between the two is exact. As the character and proportions of the foundation determine the shape and extent of the building, the latter answering precisely to the former, so must the Church answer and be the expression of its Foundation, even Christ. Particularly so as He has designed it to be His dwelling—it must be pleasing to Him who indwells it; it must worthily express His presence and personality.

(3) AS THE BRIDE BELONGS TO THE BRIDEGROOM. In no other relationship known to man is there such a sense of belonging, soul answering to soul, spirit to spirit, life to life. It constitutes an indissoluble union, a blending of two personalities as one. In such bonds as these the Church is united to Christ. For time and for eternity she knows no life apart from Him.

Are these tremendous facts causing the Church to be consciously reserved for her Lover and her Lord? Is she acknowledging herself to be supremely His? Is she drawing her life from Him? Giving her strength to Him? Is she growing in His likeness, thus to make evident to all her intimate life-union with Him?

Some time since there appeared upon the streets of Washington a person who occasioned considerable comment. Men would turn about to gaze, remarking, "What a wonderful head! No such massive head has been seen upon the streets of Washington since the days of Daniel Webster." Then they would turn again to gaze and comment: "But look at the body!" It was stunted, dwarfed, deformed. To a body such as this that wonderful head was joined. No one could think of the head apart from a body that detracted from its glory. The Great Head of the Church, possessed of a spiritually undernourished, undeveloped Body—is this the spectacle the world beholds?

Dear reader, as the definite fruit of your study of Ephesians, will you form a purpose, deep and abiding, so to live in intimate union with Him that in your life, and in the Church as far as in you lies, it shall be otherwise?

Some one has characterized a Christian as

A Mind through which Christ Thinks;
A Heart through which Christ Loves;
A Voice through which Christ Speaks;
A Hand through which Christ Helps.

How true to the believer's portrait found in Ephesians! Dear reader, your Saviour and Lord is counting upon you to be *His Very Own* in just such a life and for just such a service.